DIGGING

Boston September 2016

To Jack Topalian —

great meeting you, your son, and the inimitable Ken Davitian last month in Hollywood!

Armenians are *precious*!

Hope our paths cross again —

In great friendship —

Michael Hastings

This book is dedicated to my son, Michael, whose spirit warms my days.

ISBN 1-889833-92-4

Commonwealth Editions
an imprint of Memoirs Unlimited, Inc.
266 Cabot Street, Beverly, Massachusetts 01915
www.commonwealtheditions.com

Design by Stephen Bridges
Printed by Capital Offset Company, Concord, NH
Bound by Acme Bookbinding, Charlestown, MA

Jacket and title page: Signaling a concrete truck under Causeway Street, 2000

The Workers of Boston's Big Dig Photographs by Michael Hintlian

DIGGING

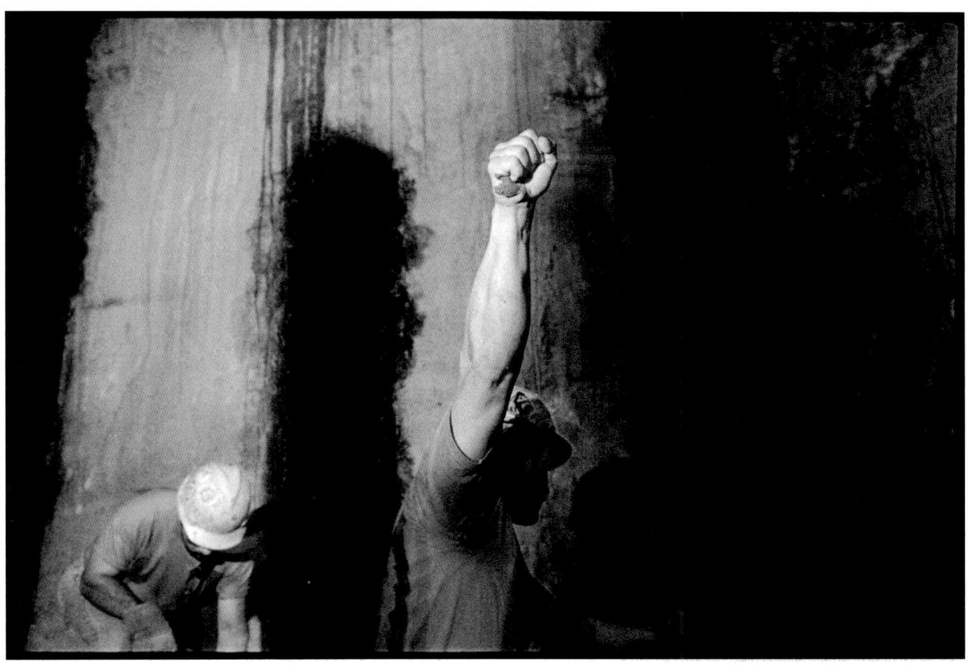

Foreword by Frederick Salvucci

Commonwealth Editions
Beverly, Massachusetts

Foreword

The Big Dig is the biggest highway construction project in the United States. Its planners' goal has been to eliminate the worst traffic bottlenecks in the nation's interstate highway system by doubling highway capacity east–west across Boston Harbor and north–south through the center of Boston. But the Big Dig is more than that, too. It is a major effort to transform the center of Boston by eliminating an ugly elevated highway that separated the core of the city from the harbor, and by reconnecting the neighborhoods of the city, both to each other and to the harbor that first gave Boston its economic life. Further, the Big Dig is an effort to replace an aging, structurally deficient elevated highway with a secure underground roadway — while maintaining traffic flow for the 200,000 vehicles essential to the city's life. It is an interstate highway project whose major goal is environmental improvement — which has avoided taking even a single house while reducing air pollution, creating twenty acres of parkland in the city center, and using the excess fill to transform a Boston Harbor Island from a rendering plant and dump location into a new park. Although designed to facilitate traffic, the Big Dig is one element of a balanced transportation plan that shifted priorities to major new links in the transit system rather than adding new interstate highways and potentially destroying several urban neighborhoods. And the Big Dig is a project that features ingenious engineering solutions to seemingly unsolvable construction problems, one that has contributed a new icon to the cityscape, a cable-stayed bridge over the Charles River.

The new structures and parks created by the Big Dig have been named for people and places that make Boston proud. The Leonard P. Zakim Bunker Hill Bridge is named for both a person and for a significant place in our country's history. Lenny Zakim was a civil rights leader who built bridges among the city's religious and ethnic groups. The Battle of Bunker Hill during the Revolutionary War was so costly to the British "victors" that they decided to evacuate the city, giving the American experiment in democracy its first real hope of victory. What was for so long called simply the "third harbor tunnel" is the new Ted Williams Tunnel,

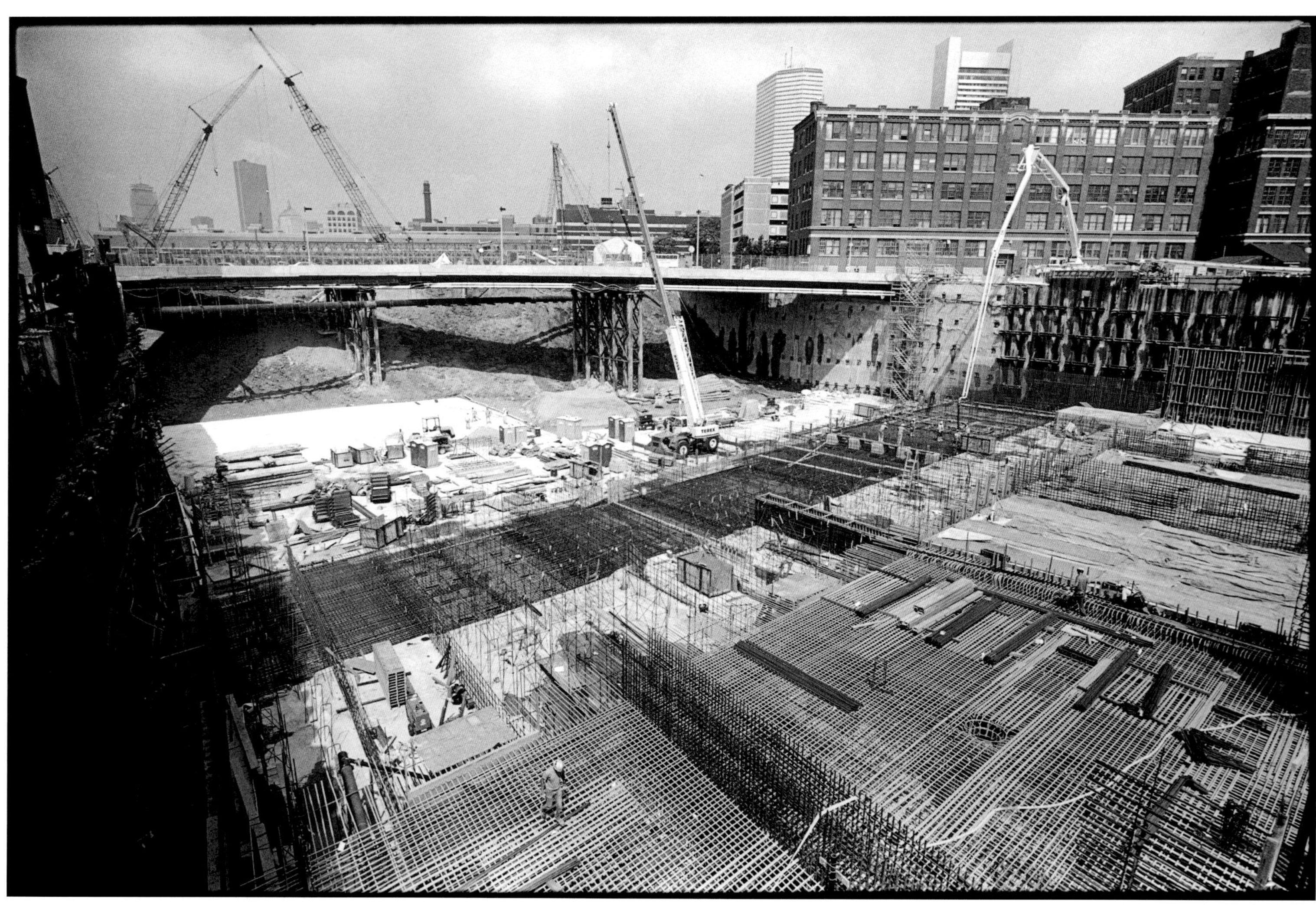

◀ Massachusetts Turnpike connector at A Street, South Boston 2000

Looking north from Broadway Bridge, South Boston 2000

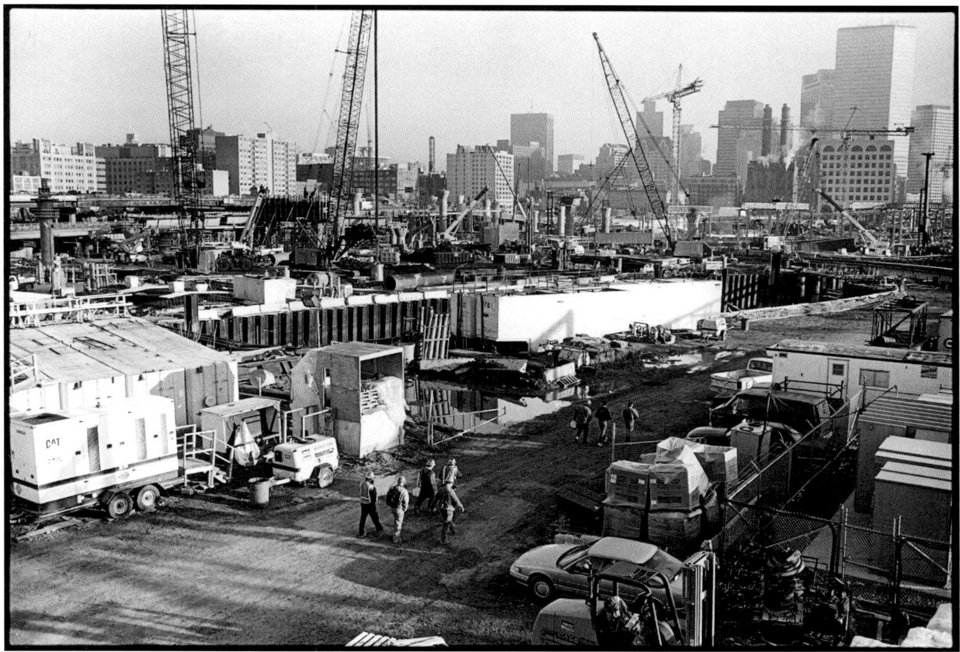

named for the famed Red Sox slugger, who gave Bostonians hope of winning pennants and World Series. The new tunnel under the city is to be named for Thomas P. "Tip" O'Neill, longtime congressman (and Speaker of the U.S. House of Representatives), who fought for decades to secure the funds to complete this part of Boston's—and the nation's—interstate system. The surface parks, the green space, that are replacing the ugly elevated Central Artery are dedicated to the memory of Rose Fitzgerald Kennedy, daughter of John F. Fitzgerald, Boston's first Irish-American mayor, and mother of President John F. Kennedy and Senators Robert F. and Edward M. Kennedy. It was Ted Kennedy who consolidated the political effort in the Senate to secure the completion of this landmark project.

By the time you read this book, most of this work on the multibillion-dollar Big Dig will be complete, and construction of the Rose Kennedy Greenway will be underway, to embellish the surface area that has been in the shadow of an elevated highway for fifty years. Michael Hintlian's stunning photography reminds us that, at its core, the project has been about construction workers using their muscle and brains to create an engineering marvel. Years ago, in his book *Christ in Concrete*, Pietro Di Donato captured the spirit of a young man whose father was killed on a dangerous construction job and who then does the same kind of work to help his widowed mother survive. Just as Di Donato captured in words the young worker's pride and pain, even the ache in his back that reminds him all night of that day's work, so Michael Hintlian has captured in photographs both the acrobatic poetry in motion of Big Dig workers and the sheer bone-chilling ache involved in the work. At the level of the individual worker, we see the skill, brains, and muscle needed to succeed at tasks that seem impossible. Hintlian has given us a unique opportunity to sense how this project looked to the workers who built it — underground, in the mud, or a hundred feet in the air on the Zakim Bridge.

The labor unions, whose apprenticeship programs enable these skills to be passed on, and who have worked for over a hundred years to organize and fight for better benefits and wages for workers and their families, have provided financial support to help publish this unique book, to give us all a chance to see the project as they saw it. Hintlian's photographs celebrate their irreplaceable contribution, and give us all a chance to appreciate it.

Frederick Salvucci

July 2004

Fred Salvucci served as Massachusetts Secretary of Transportation during the twelve years Michael Dukakis was governor, and as transportation advisor to Boston Mayor Kevin White prior to that. During those sixteen years, he worked to conceptualize the Big Dig and to secure its environmental permits and funding. He was educated at the Boston Latin School and received bachelor's and master's degrees in civil engineering from MIT. Prior to that, Salvucci served an apprenticeship in the Bricklayers, Masons & Plasterers' International Union of America. Almost all his relatives are or were construction workers.

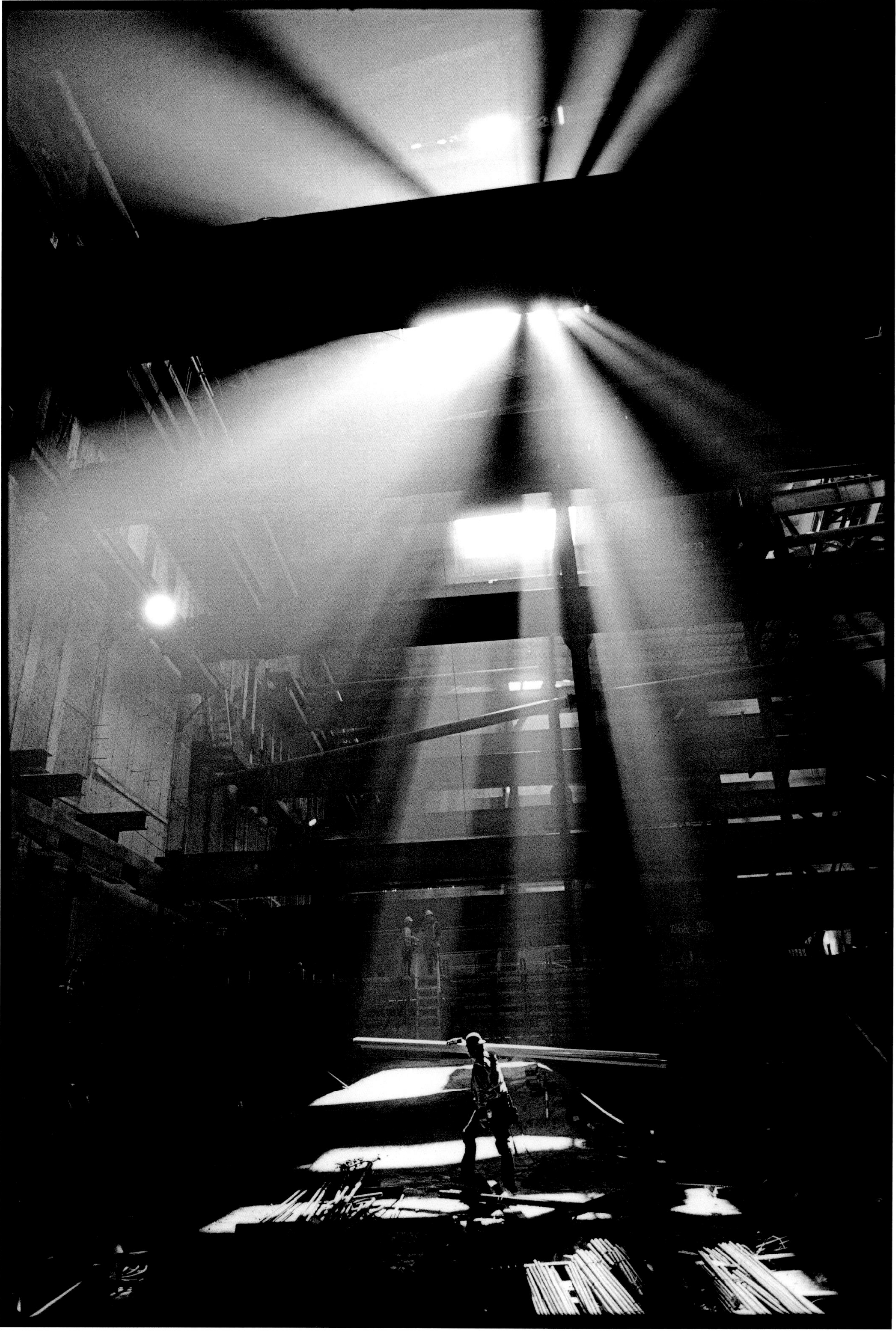

Photographer's notes

Late in 1996 I was in downtown Boston shooting when I came upon a small crew of ironworkers making rebar cages. I made no connection to what they were doing and did not think much about it. Later that same morning I saw spray-painted diagrams on the brick sidewalks of State Street detailing the structure of the utilities buried below. Then it struck me: the Big Dig was about to begin.

My immediate instinct was to find a way to get close to this project and to shoot it. I was drawn to the massive scale, and to the outrageous feat of burying several miles of eight-lane highway under the center of this major American city. But what really caught my imagination were the tradesmen and women. I wanted to document their daily work: the dirt shoveled by hand, the hundreds of thousands of welds, the whole handmade nature of the project.

The Artery has not been an easy subject to penetrate, and my access to the sites has been self-granted. I started shooting the project in early 1997, and for the first two years I was chased out of the sites every time I showed up. To my advantage, the project was so big that I could walk a block or two and enter yet another site and continue to work. Eventually supervisors got used to me, or they tired of shooing me out. By the third year I was a familiar and accepted part of the scenery to both workers and supervision. I was able to work almost unnoticed. Blending in and being accepted allowed me to work as close as I needed. I was able to move in rhythm with the workers and shoot as they shoveled, welded, nailed, and wrestled with this thing.

The Artery project is probably the most hostile environment in which I have ever worked: mud, clouds of dust, splashing concrete, an oily mist in the air, subzero temperatures in winter, and summer heat. The gritty, hard-working, sweaty atmosphere was overwhelmingly without color. The transitory nature of the project and the strong contrast of dark and light lent itself to black-and-white film.

Before any digging began, the trades spent four years relocating twenty-nine miles of utility lines that were in the path of the project. Once that was done, steel columns were sunk into the ground to bedrock at depths of up to 120 feet in places. These beams formed the walls of the new tunnel as well as temporary support for the existing elevated highway, which was to be severed from its foundation to make way for digging the tunnel. With the walls in place, the actual digging of the tunnel began.

As soil between the tunnel walls was removed, cross supports were installed to hold the walls in place as excavation went deeper. When the design depth was reached, reinforced concrete was poured to create the tunnel floor. Many of these concrete pours took more than twelve hours and used well over a hundred trucks of concrete. Asphalt or concrete roadbeds were laid over the concrete foundation, and utilities and ventilations systems were installed around and above. The final step to complete the tunnel box was to install the roof beams and top them with reinforced concrete. Over 5,000 workers were responsible for the more than half a million truckloads of dirt excavated, the nearly four million cubic yards of concrete poured, the setting of over five miles of reinforcing steel in the walls, and hand-wiring over 200,000 miles of wire and 5,000 miles of fiber-optic cable. To bring fresh air into the tunnel, seven ventilation buildings were built along its length, with an intricate network of ductwork making it one of the largest highway vent systems in the world.

Once these structures were in place, the tunnels were ready for traffic. On a cold December morning in 2003, a small ceremony marked the last car traveling over the old highway, the road was closed, and traffic was redirected into the new tunnel. Watching this simple transition was a bittersweet anticlimax. After years of so much intense work, I felt a certain sadness.

I have tried to make photographs that are a tribute to the individuals who worked on the project, as well as a documentary of a major urban infrastructure project. The project has changed me as a photographer perhaps as much as it has changed this city. I have come to see the deeper rewards of shooting from an inner place where thought cannot interfere and the heart knows its own.

Michael Hintlian
July 2004

The following men lost their lives at work on the Central Artery/Tunnel Project:
John Hegarty, piledriver, Local 56: March 11, 1998
Fook Kan, carpenter, Local 33: August 16, 1999
Lonnie Avant, operating engineer, Local 4: March 24, 2003

◀ Carpenter carrying lumber
under Haymarket
2001

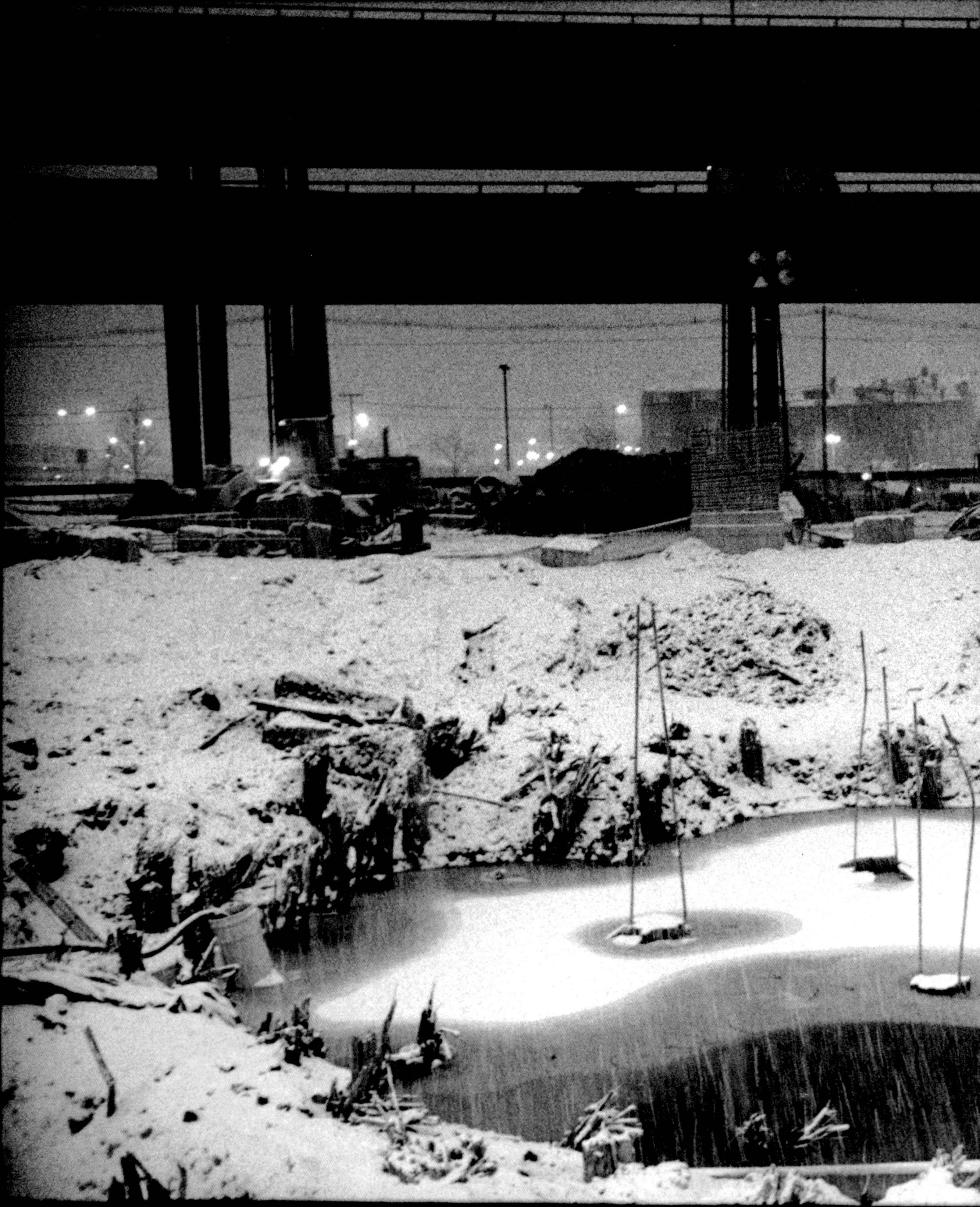

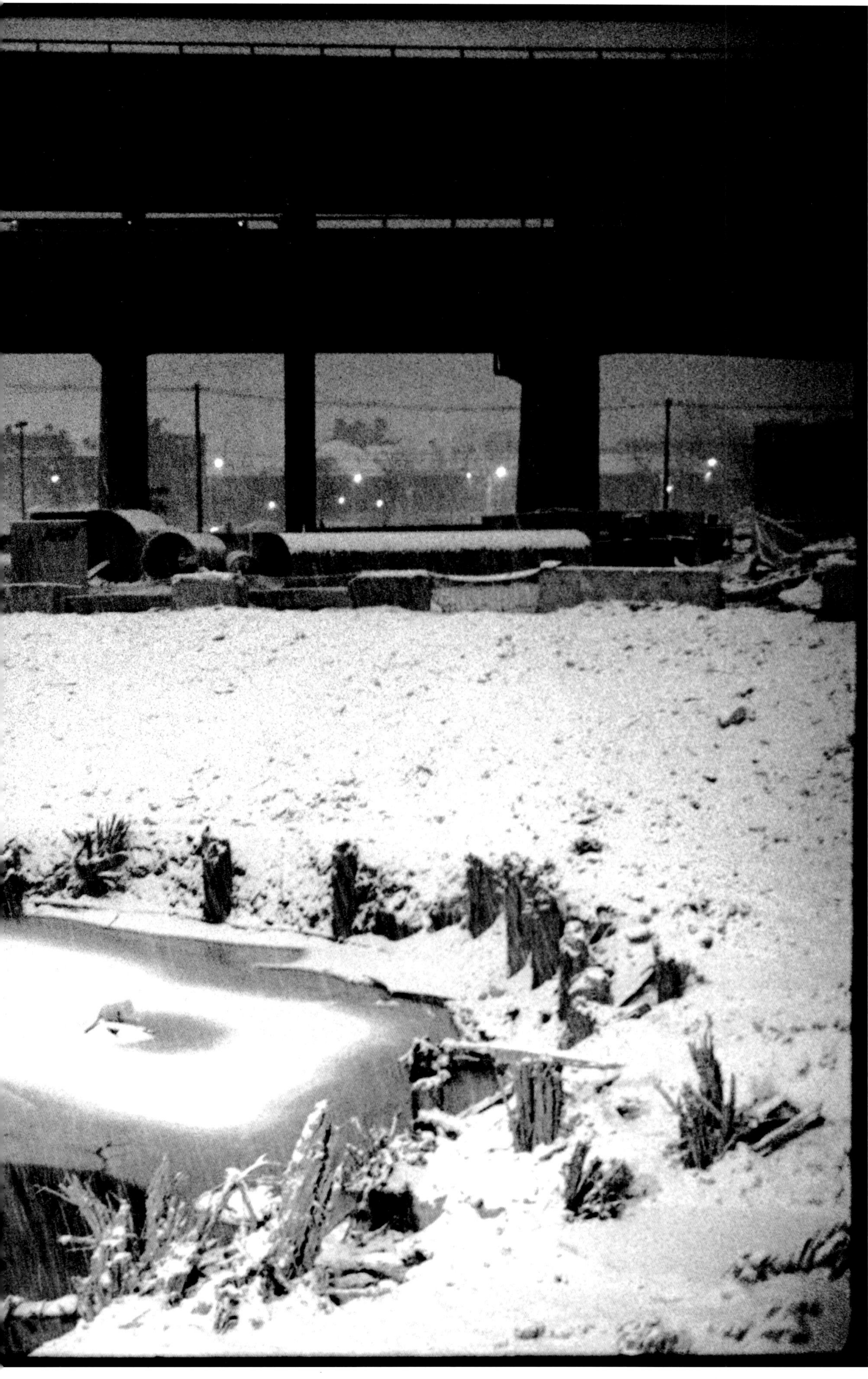

Footing for column, Leverett
Connector, Charlestown
1999

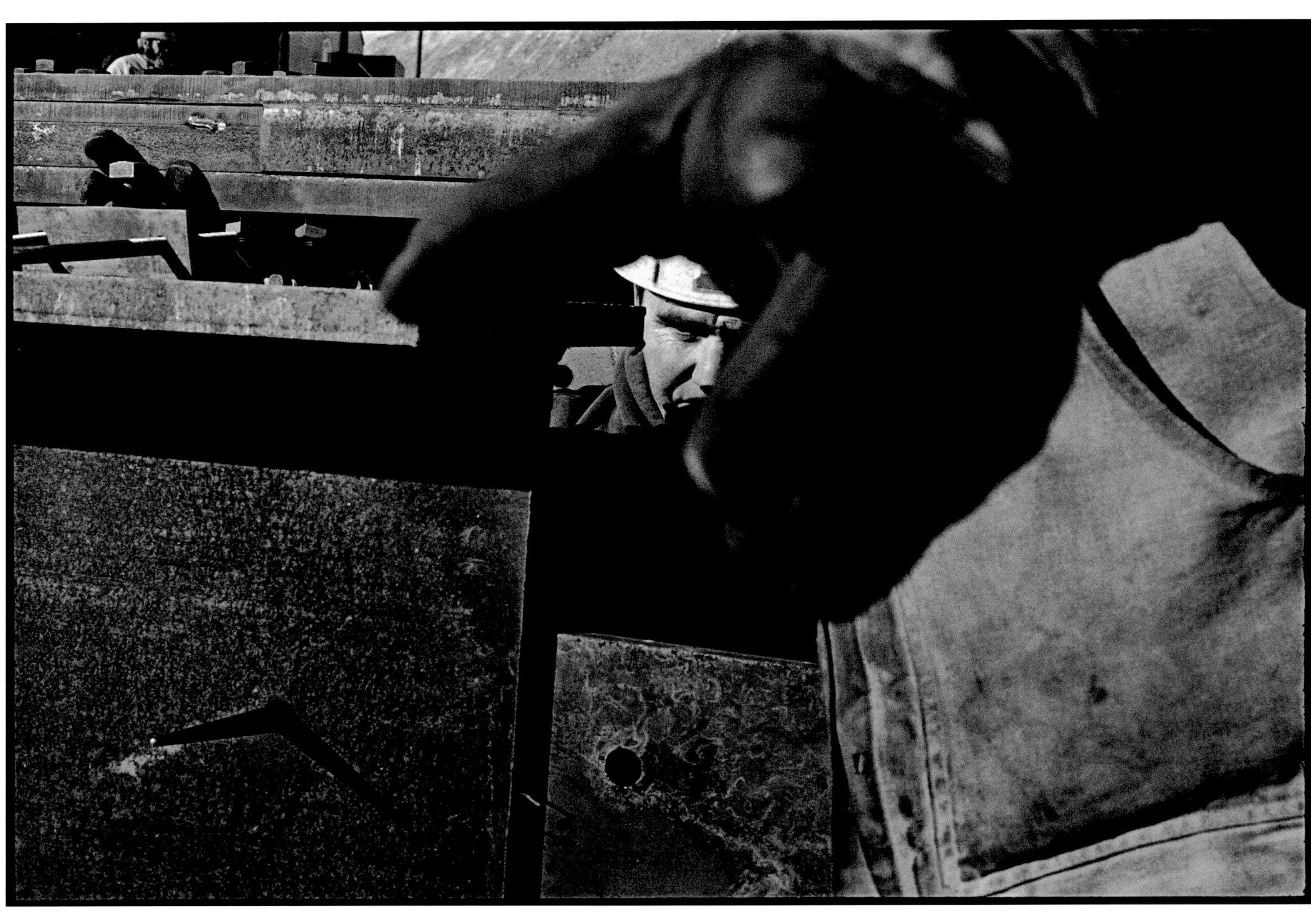

Soldier pile pre-assembly,
Everett staging yard
1997

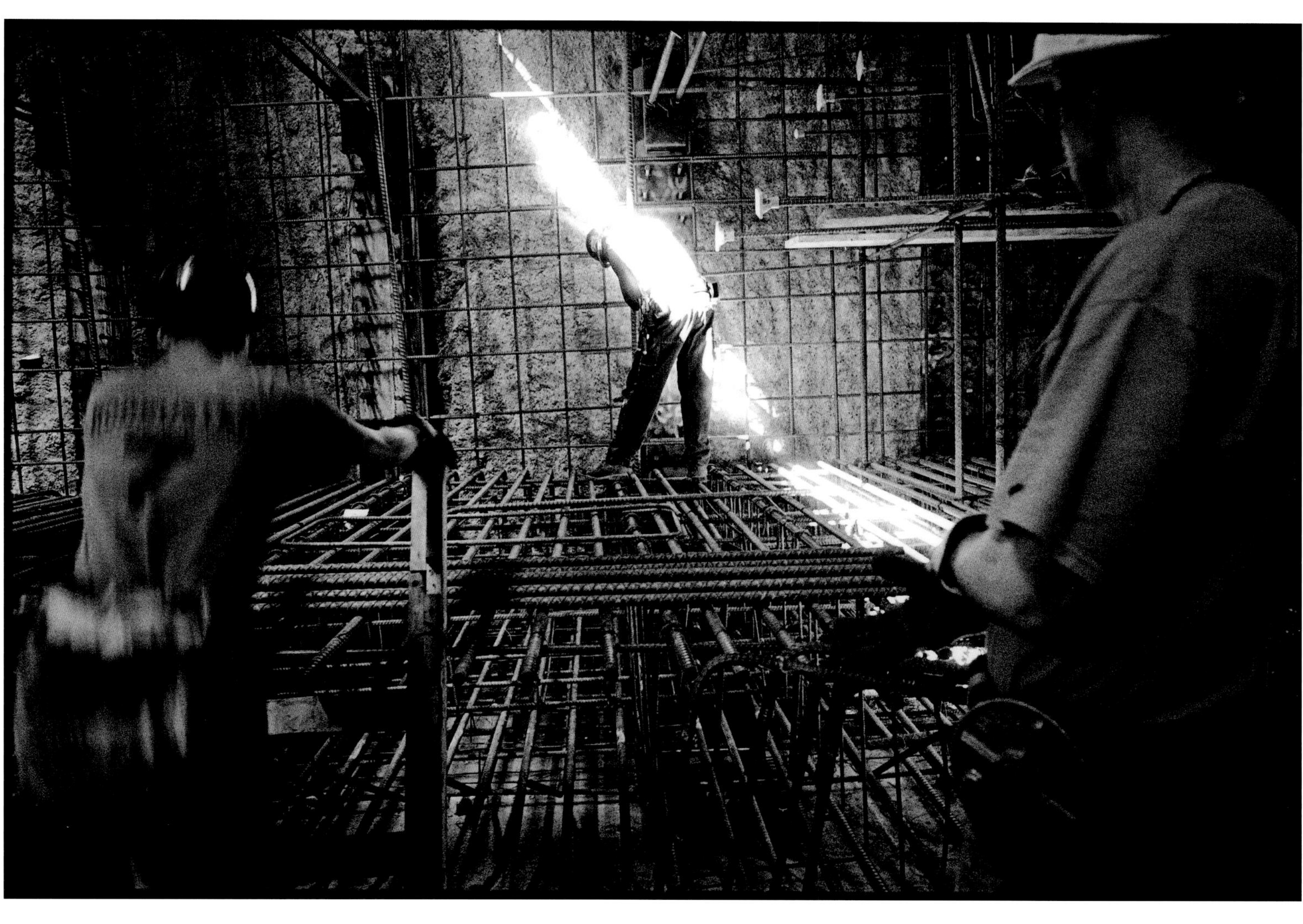

Rebar and sunlight under
Causeway Street
2001

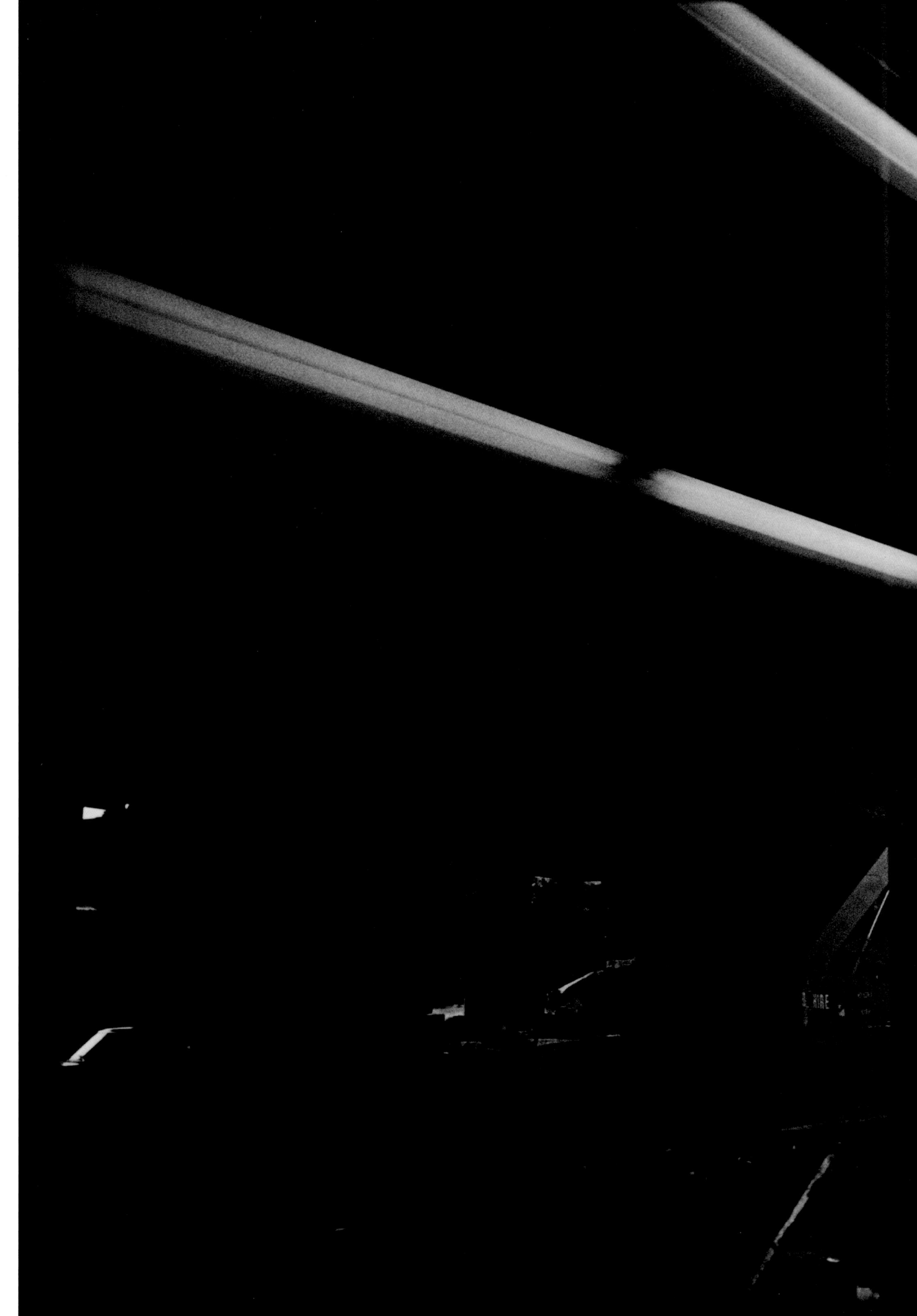

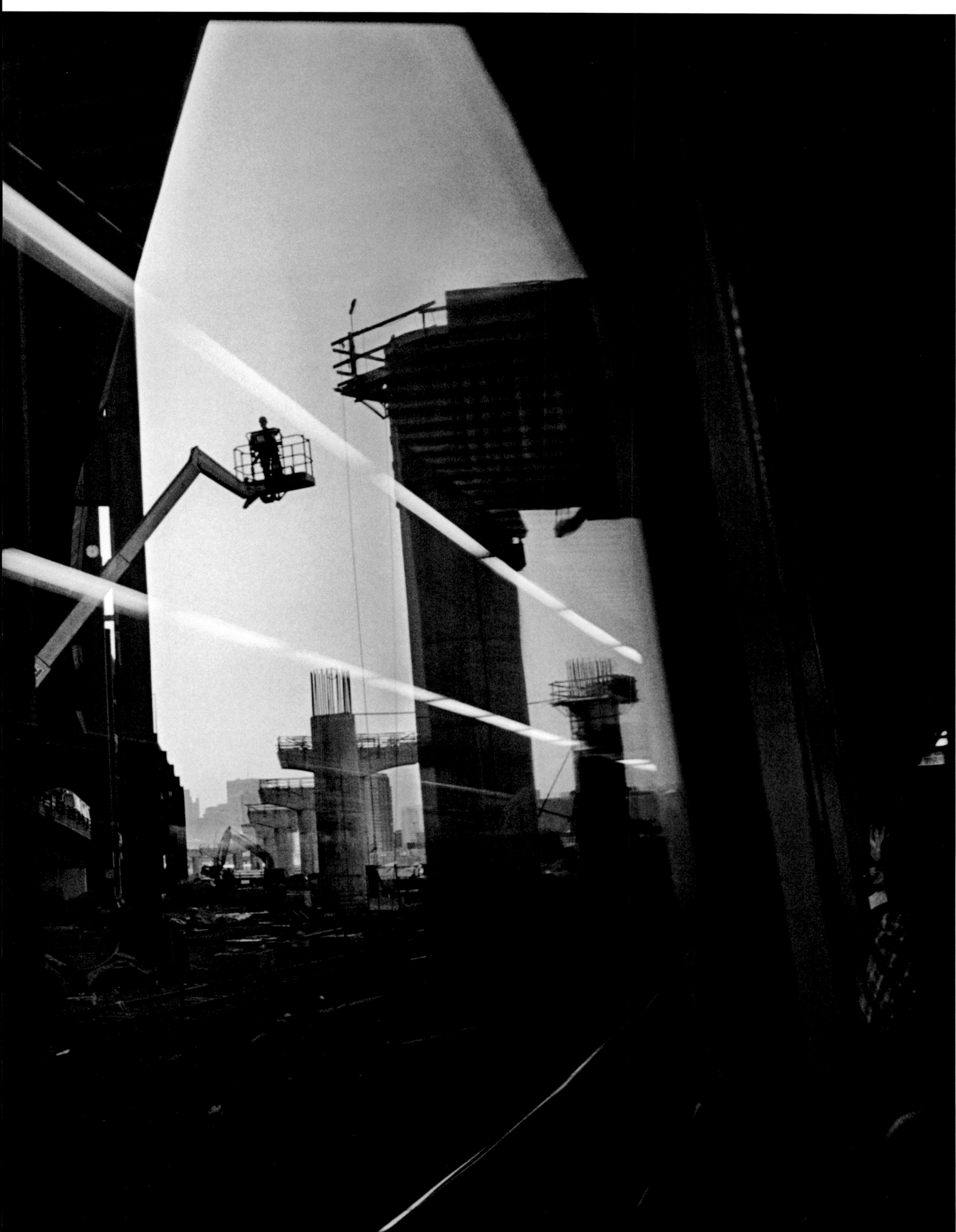

◄ Leverett Connector support columns, looking south from a commuter rail car, Charlestown
1998

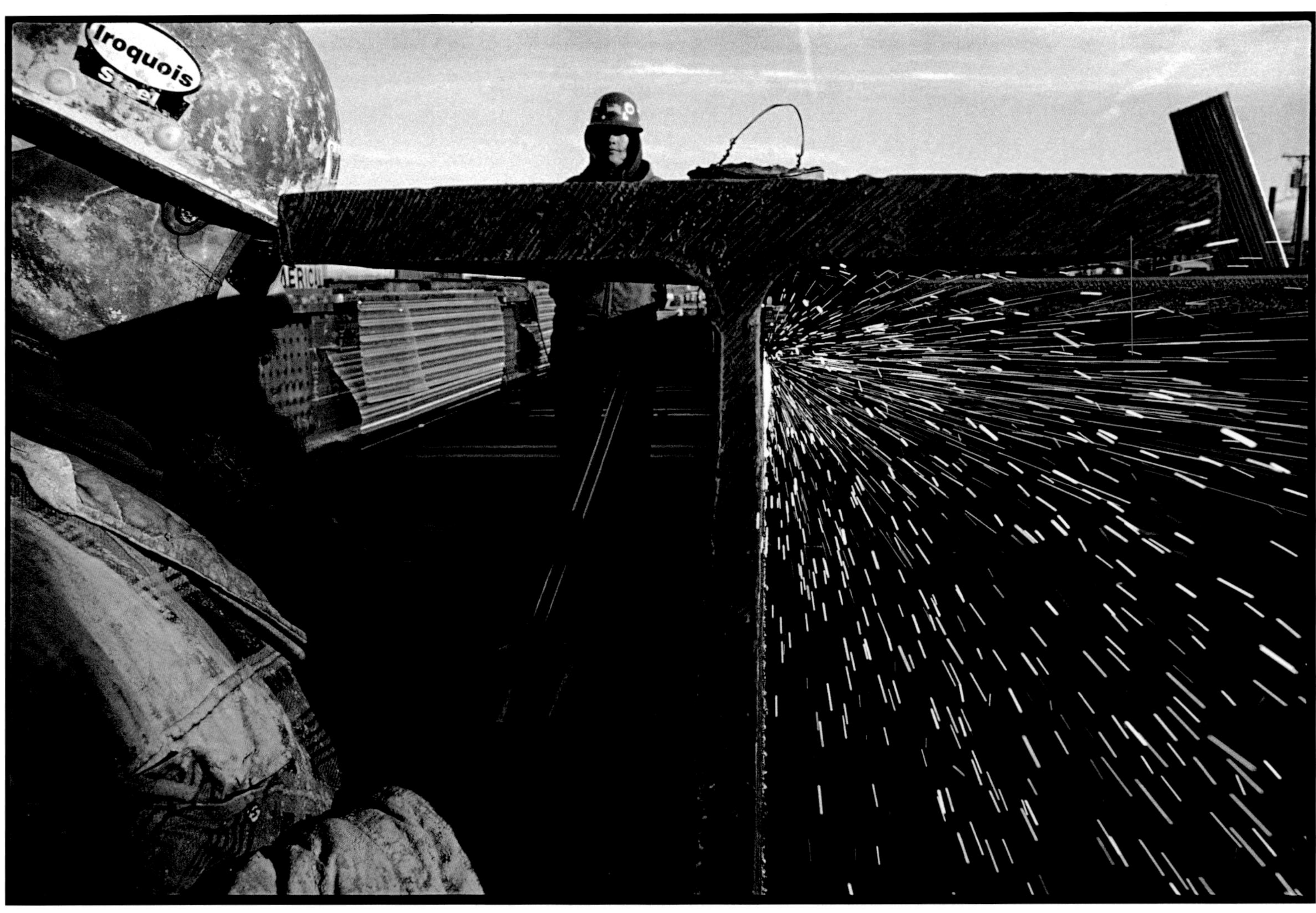

Cuttting torch and soldier pile,
Everett pre-assembly yard
1997

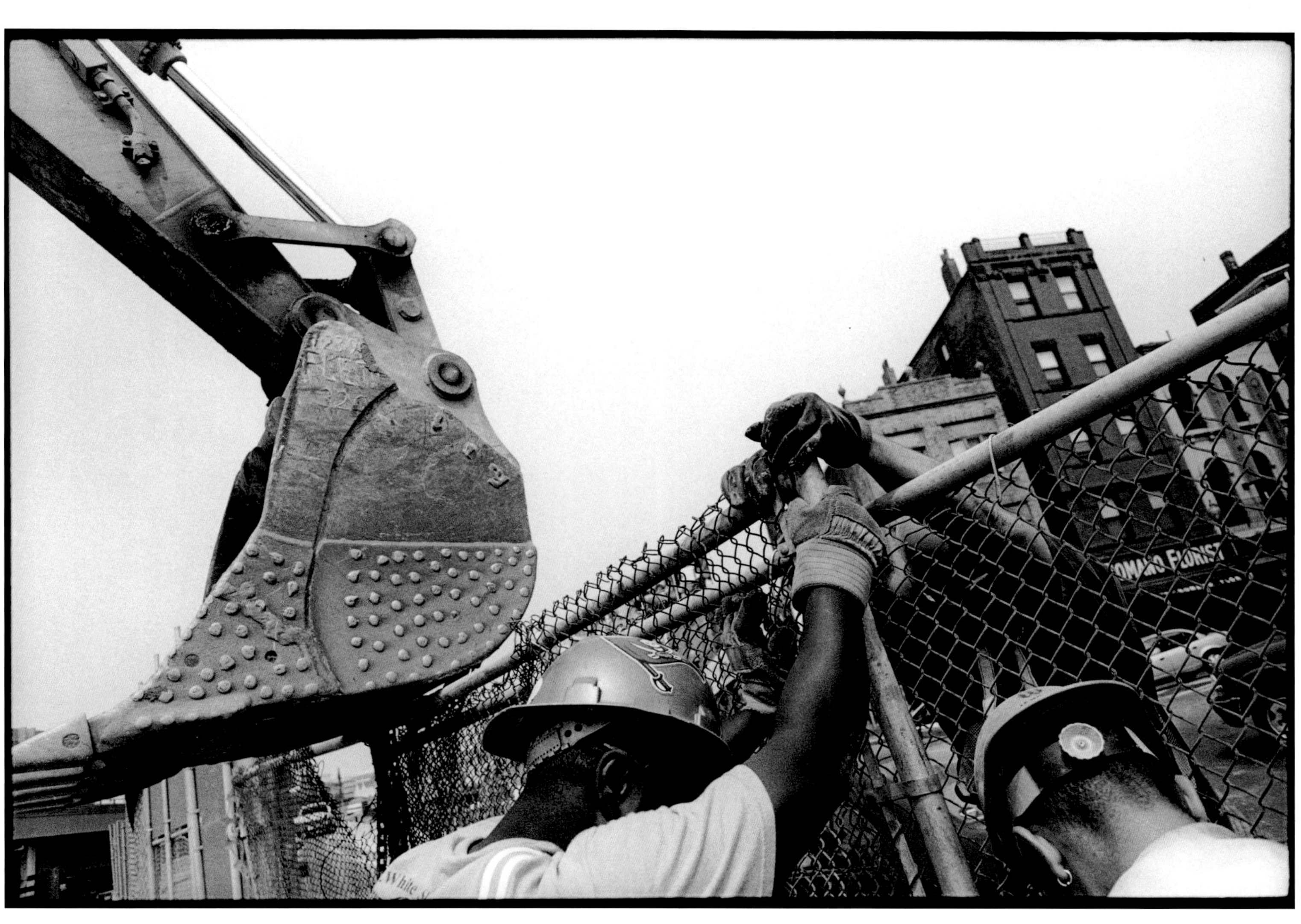

Moving a Jersey barrier,
North End
2001

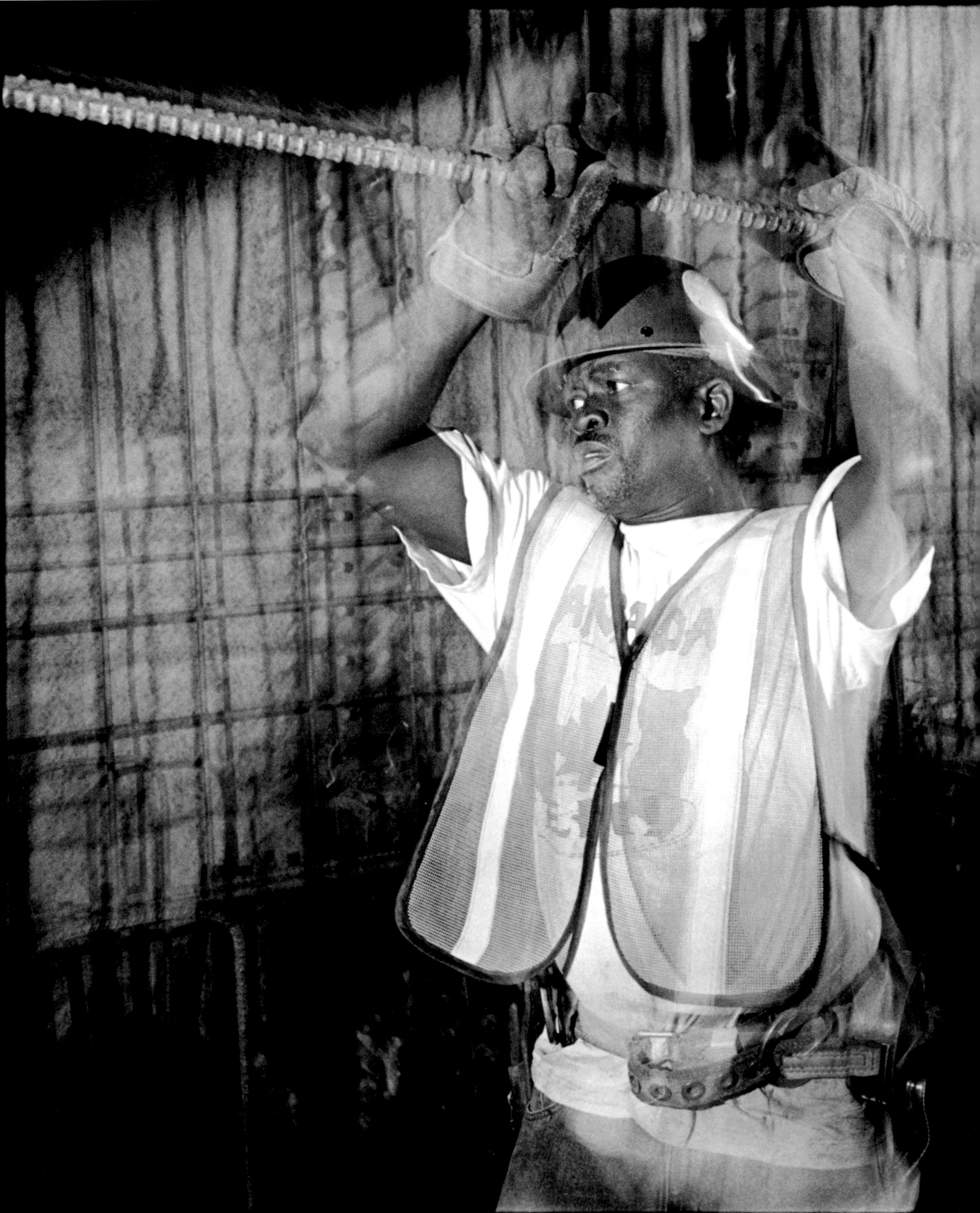

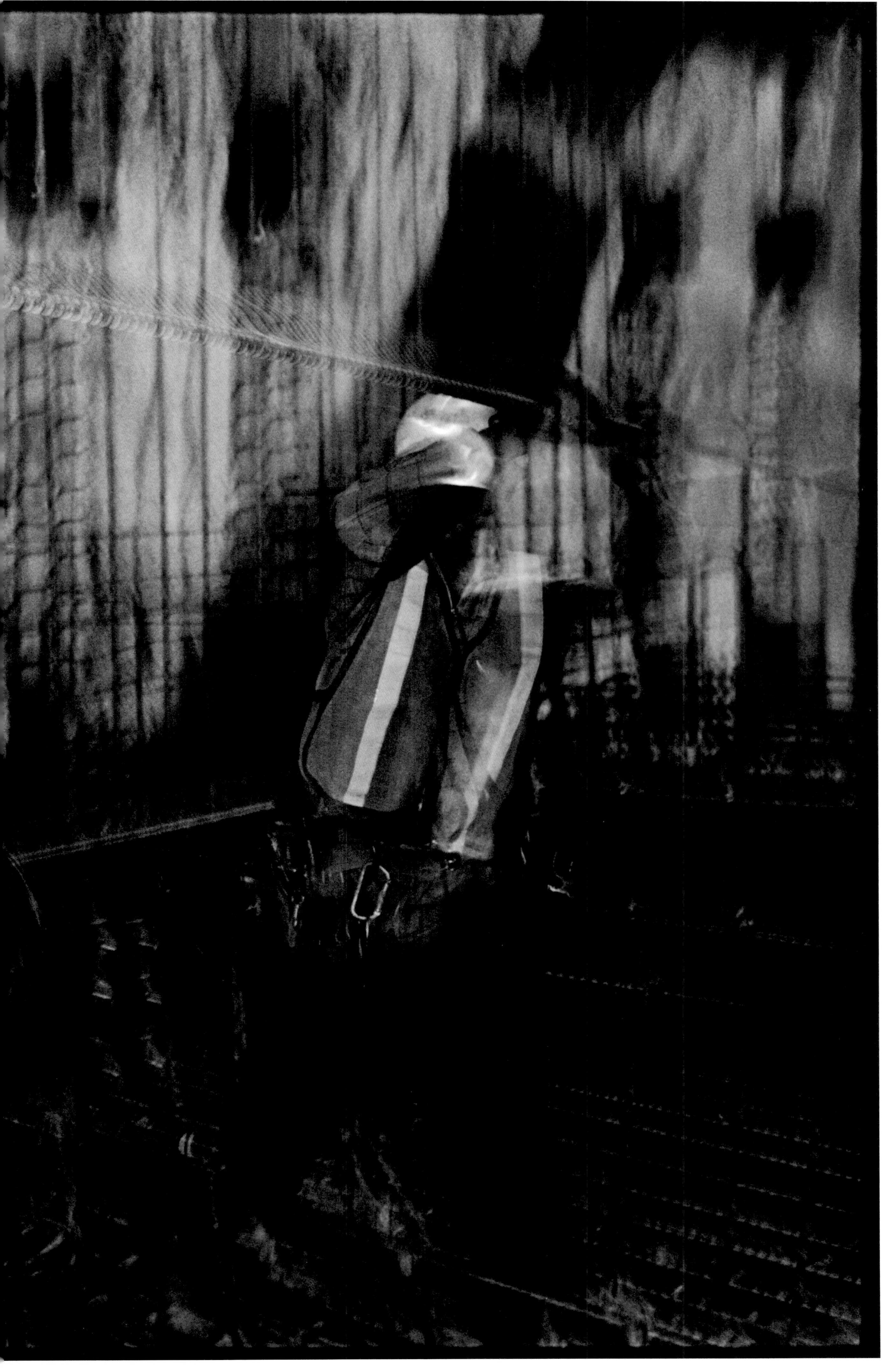

◀ Raising rebar under Haymarket
2000

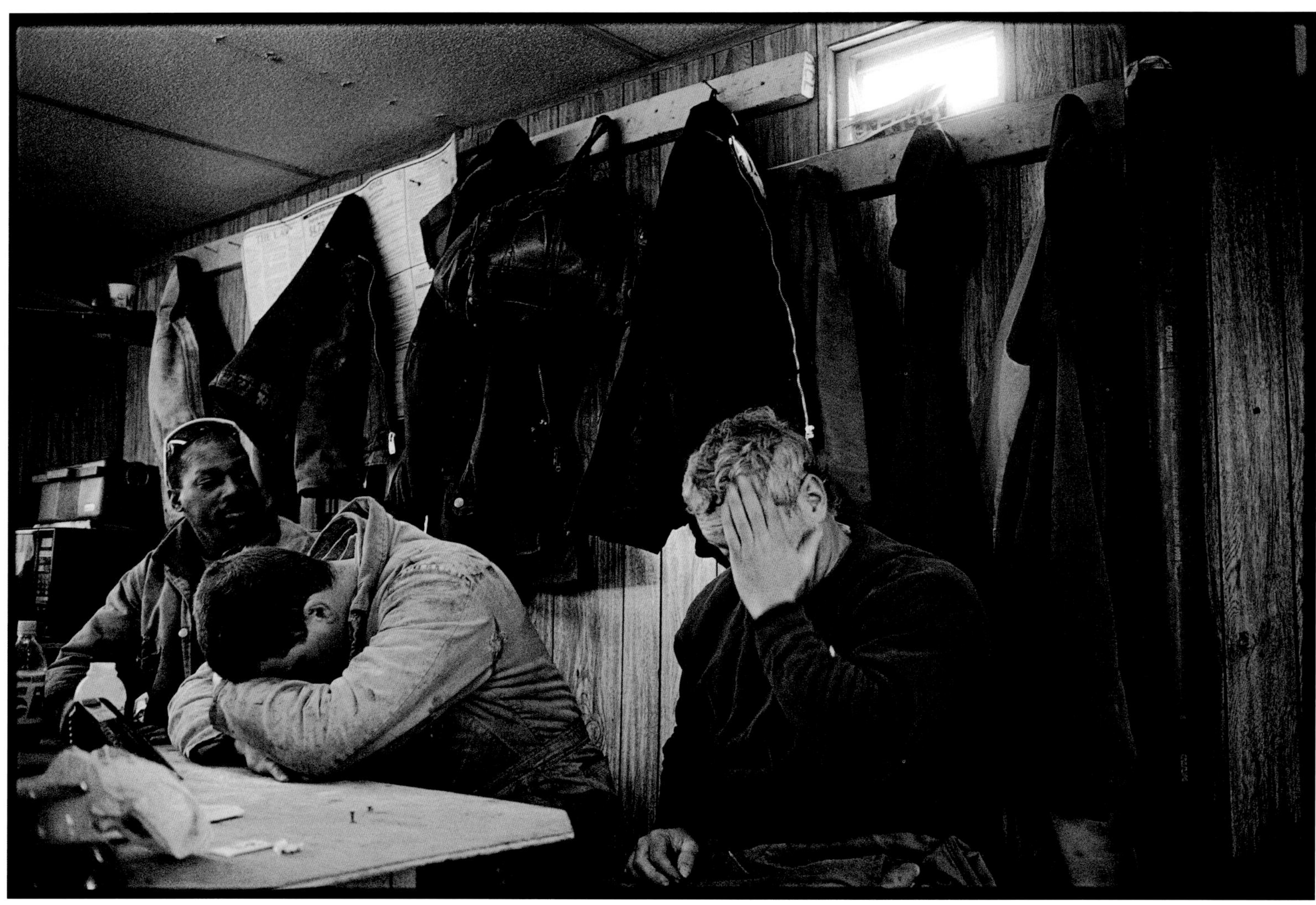

Morning break,
iron workers' shack
winter 1997

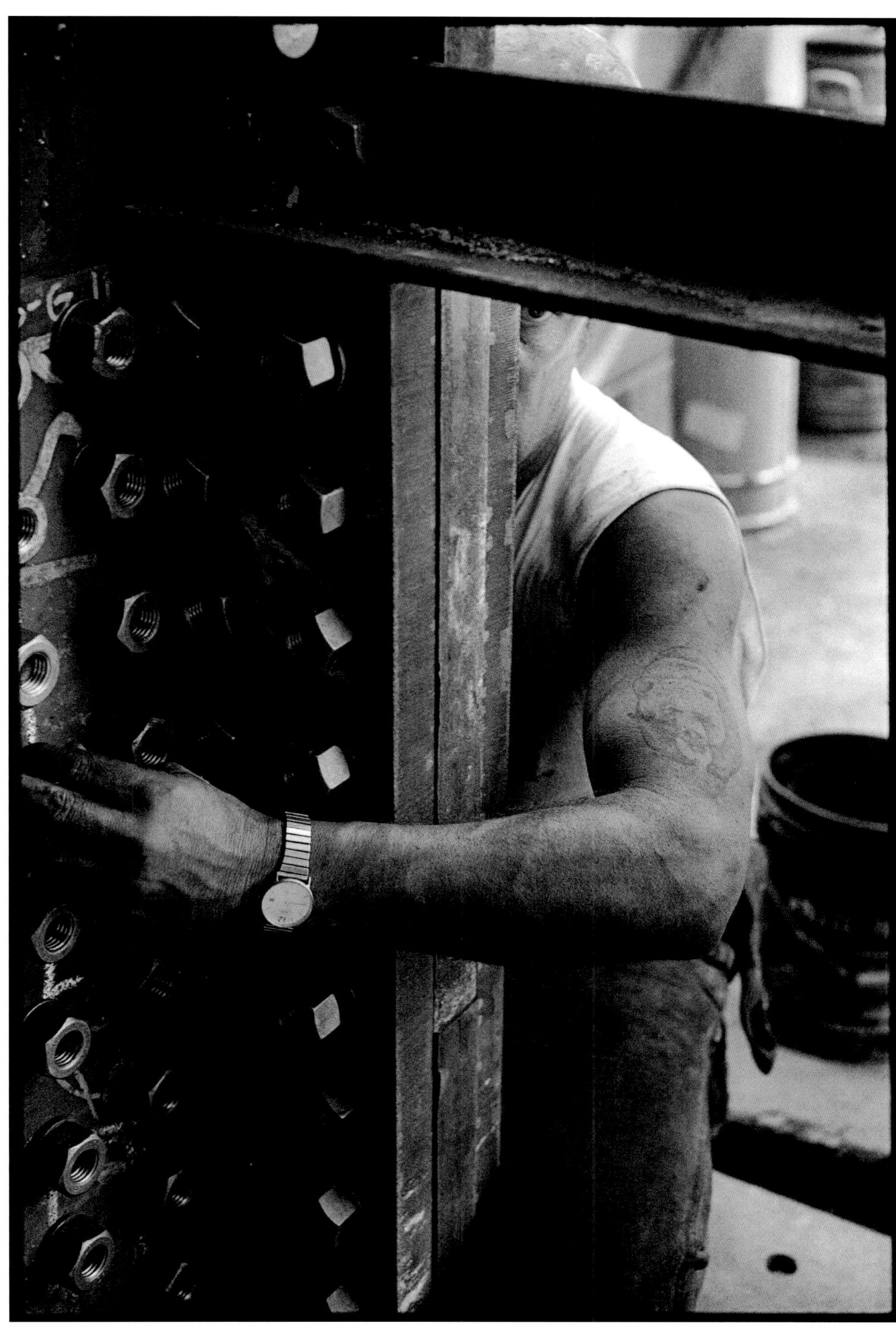

Splicing soldier pile under the
existing artery, State Street
1997

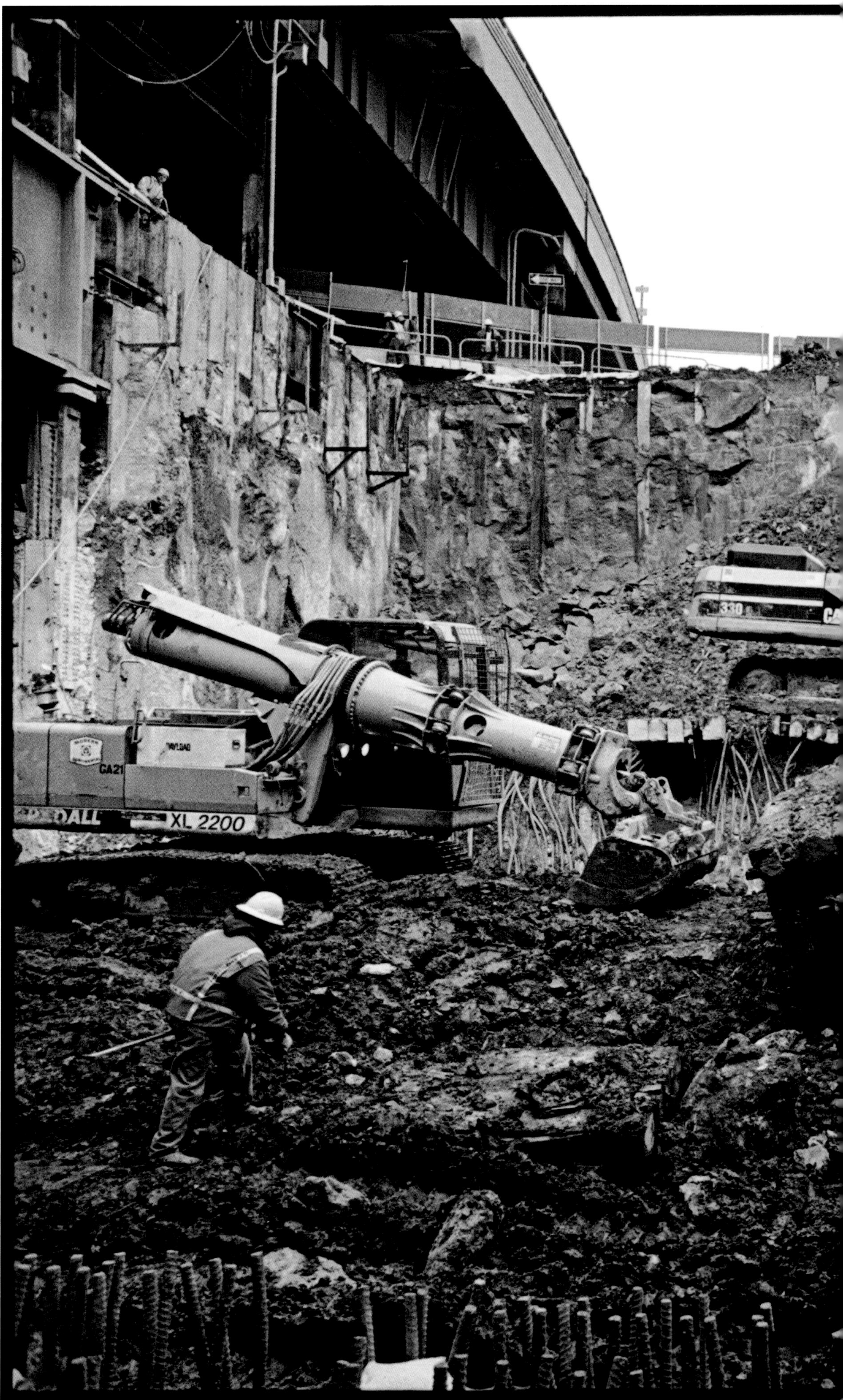

Digging around the Blue Line
tube, Atlantic Avenue and
State Street
2000

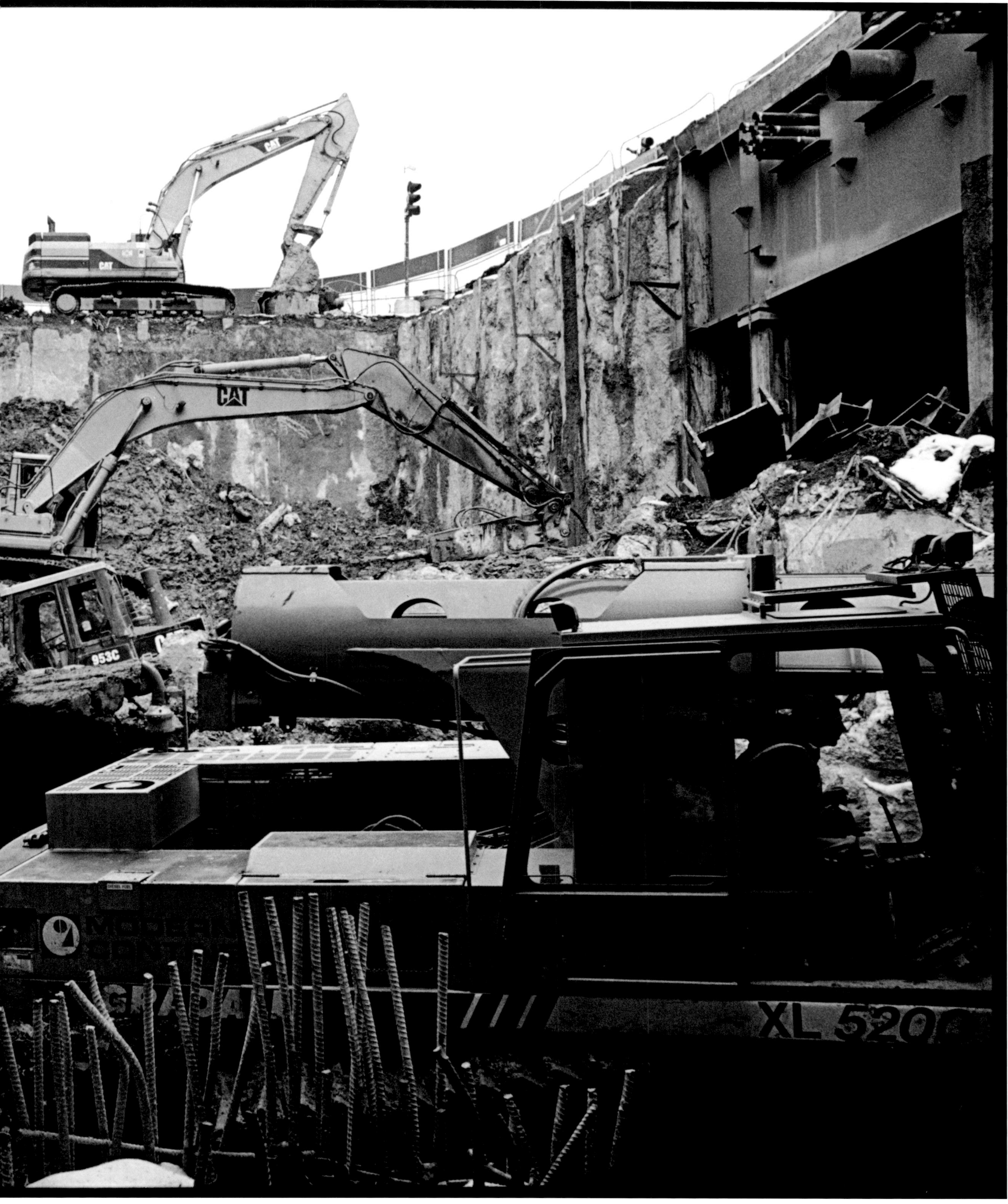
CAT
CAT
953C
XL 520

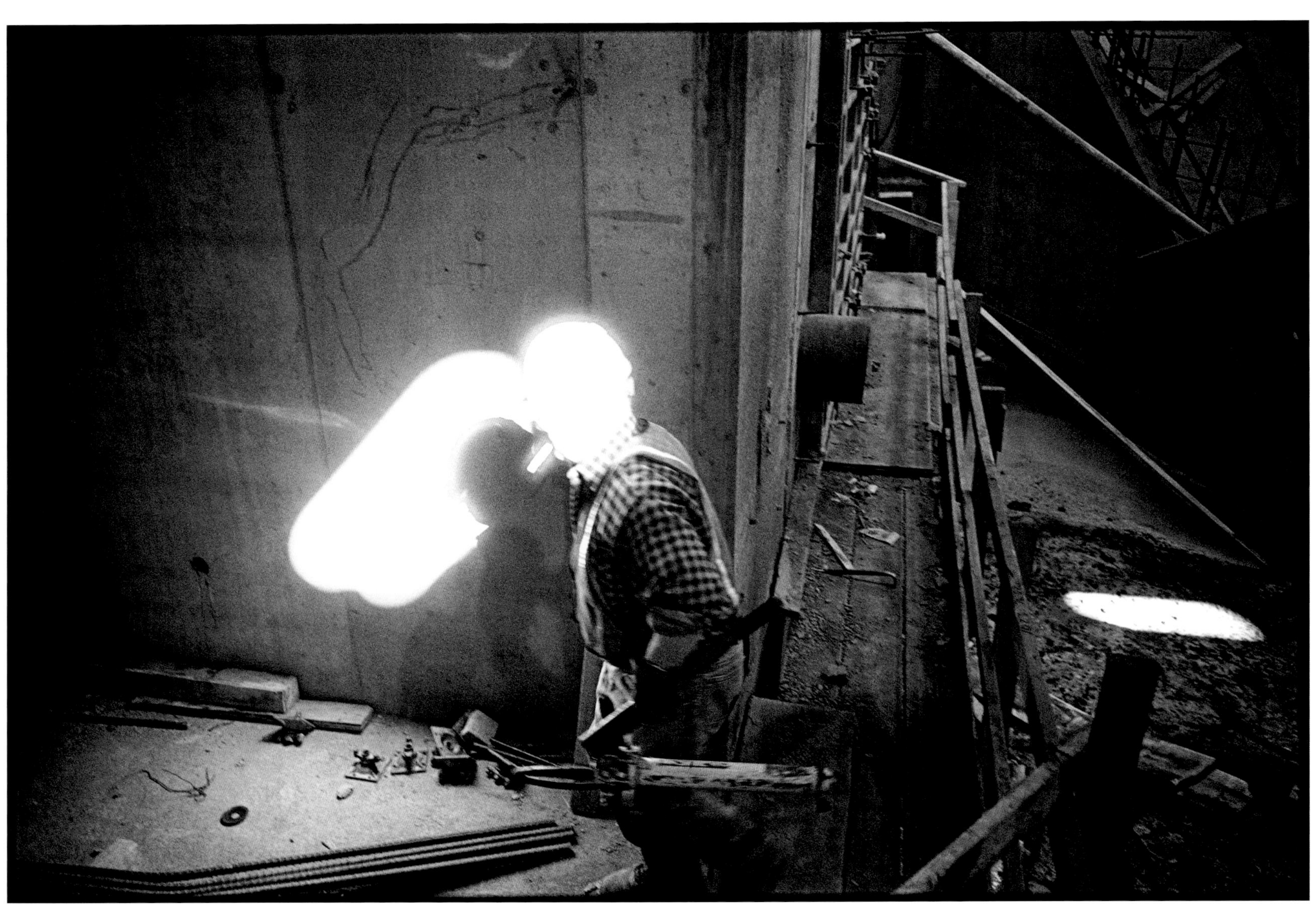

Tunnel near Haymarket
2001

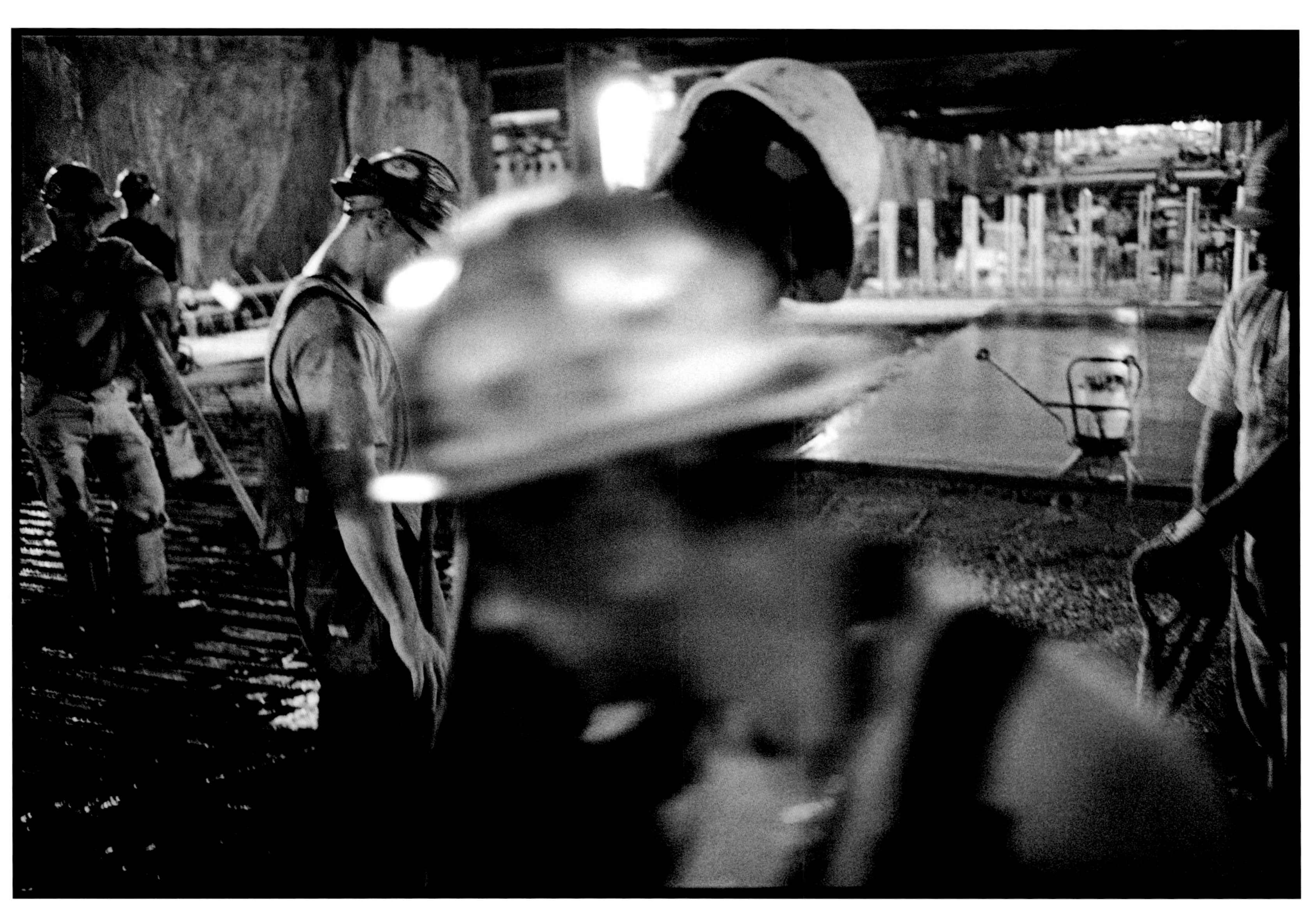

Pouring concrete under
North Washington Street
2001

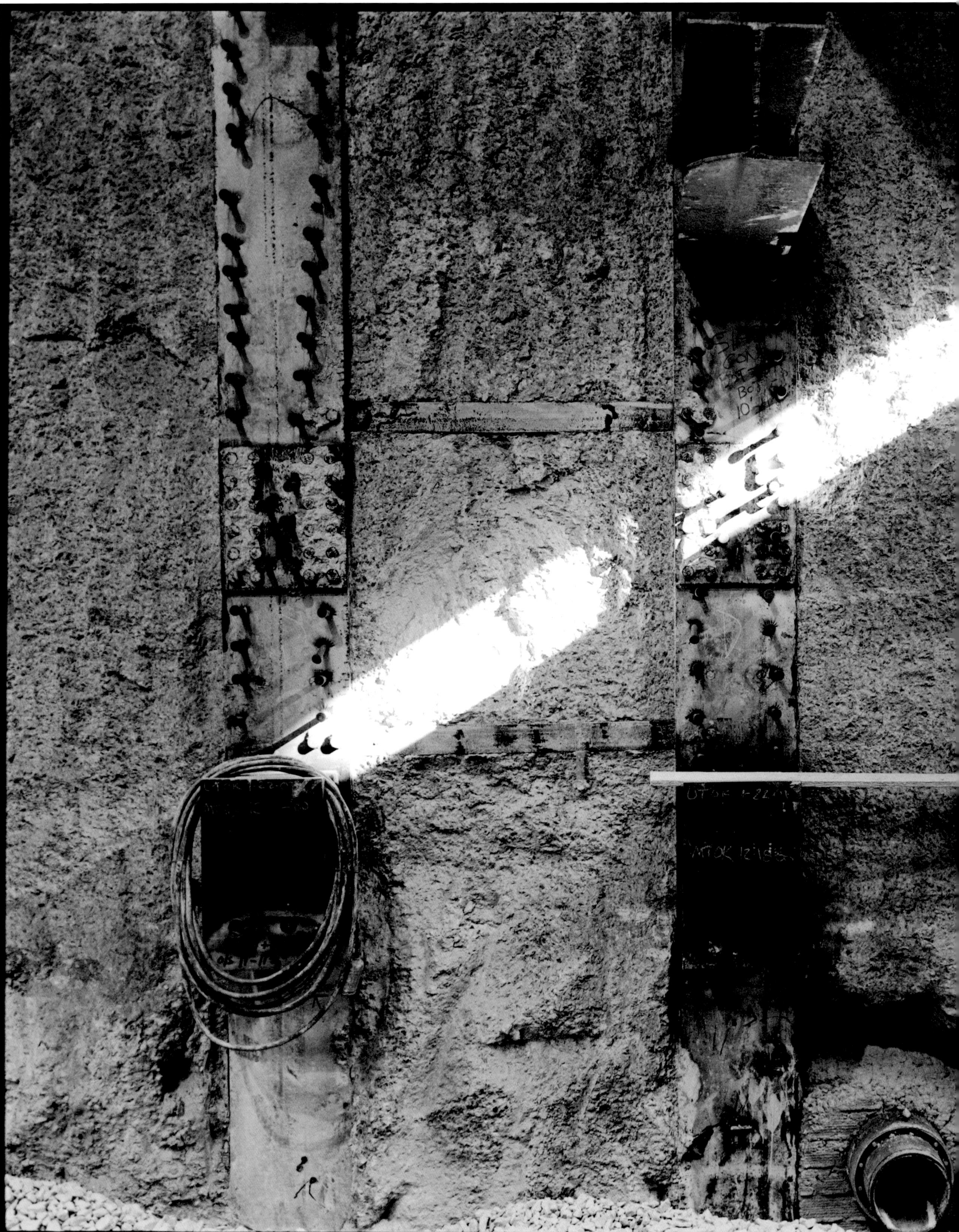

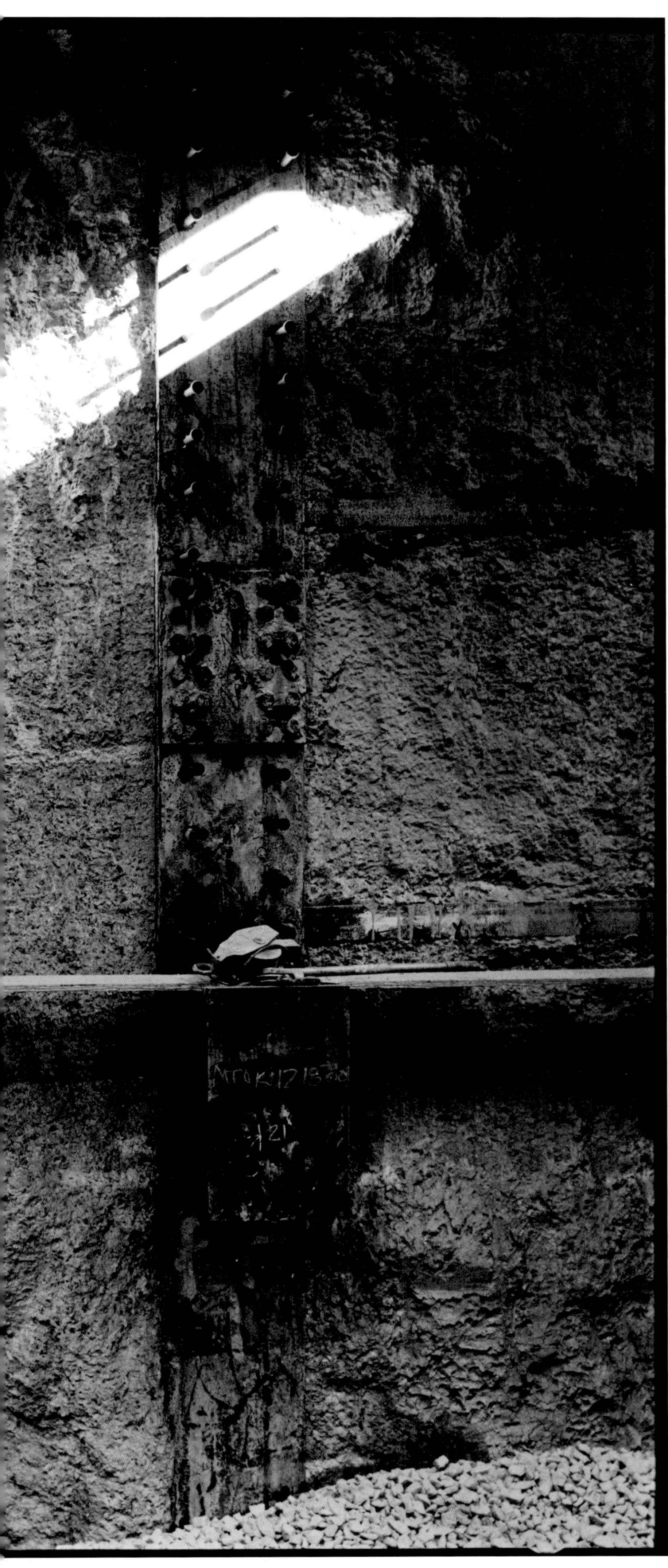

Slurry wall under
Hanover Street
2001

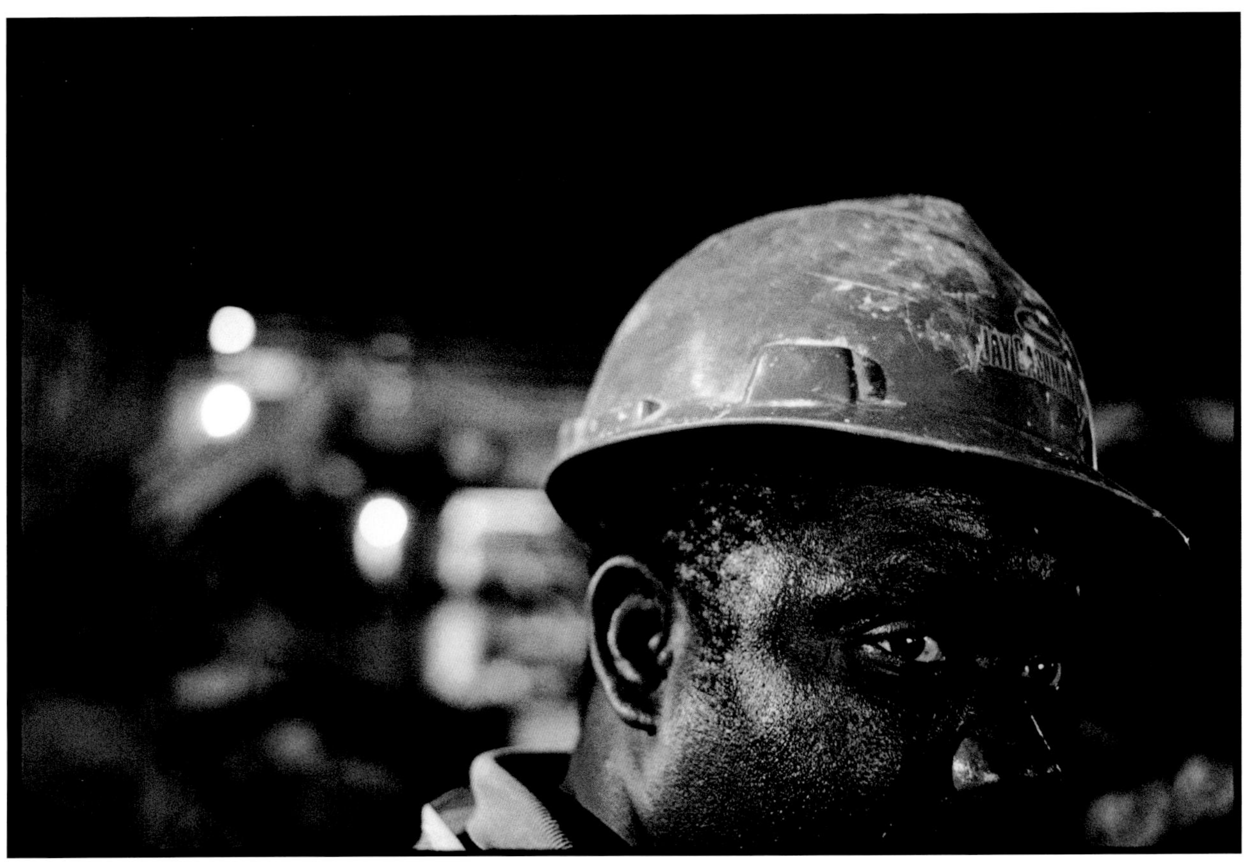

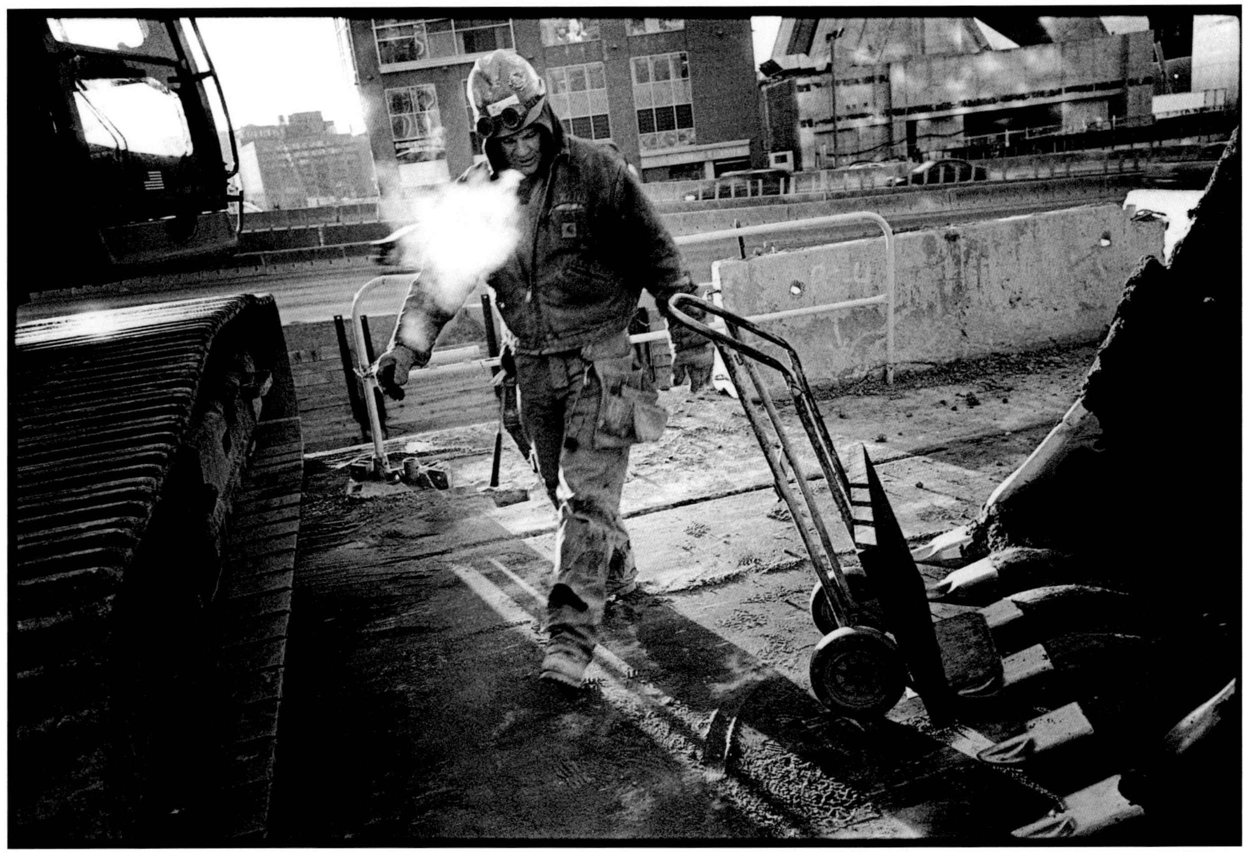

Near Causeway Street
2001

High Street
winter 2003

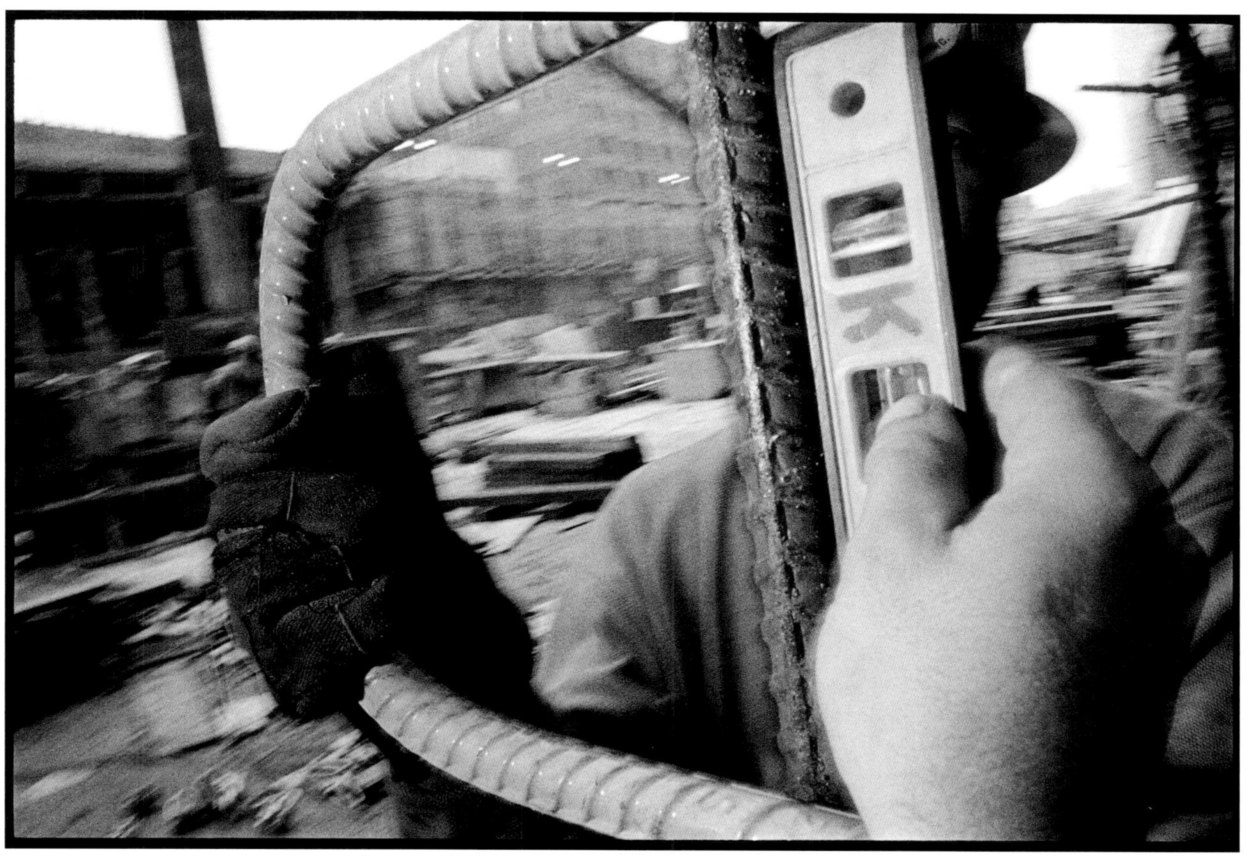

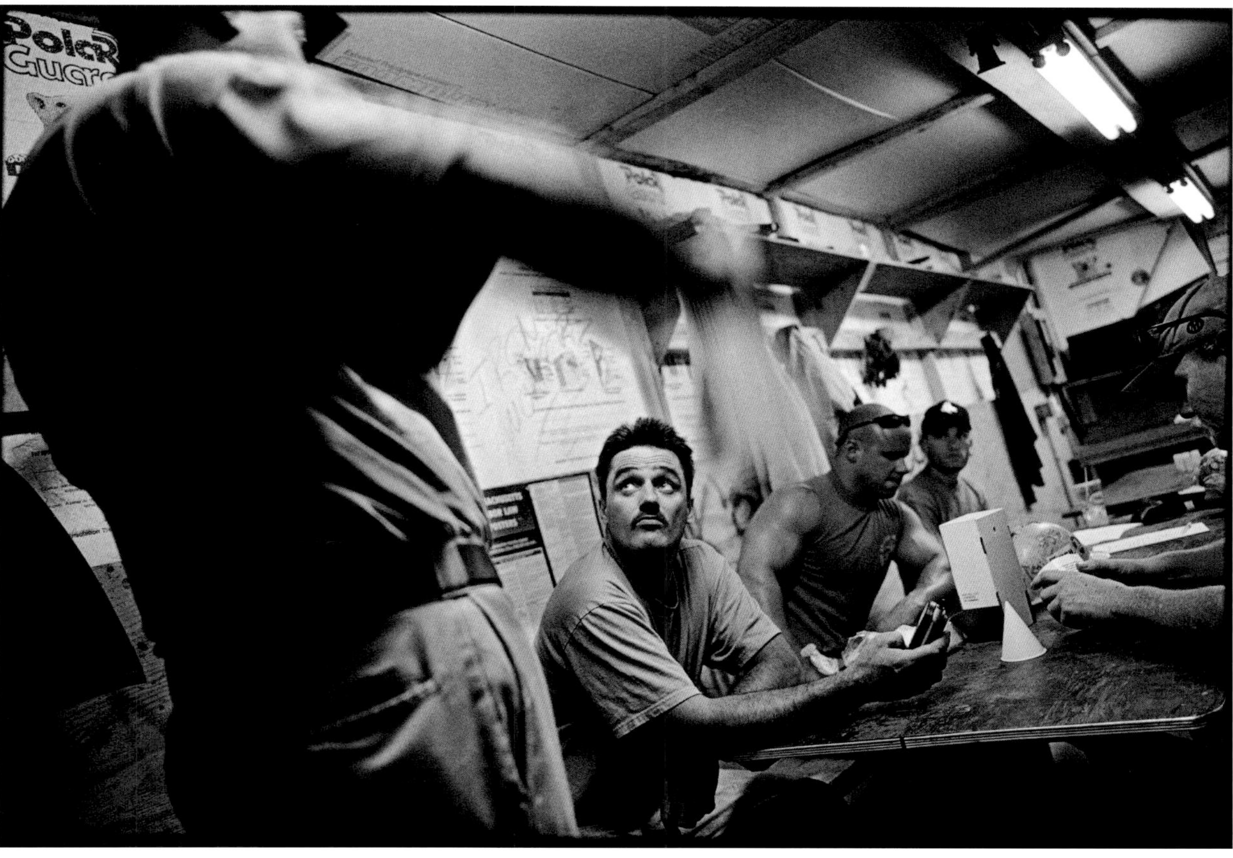

Torpedo level, near High Street
2003

Safety meeting
2002

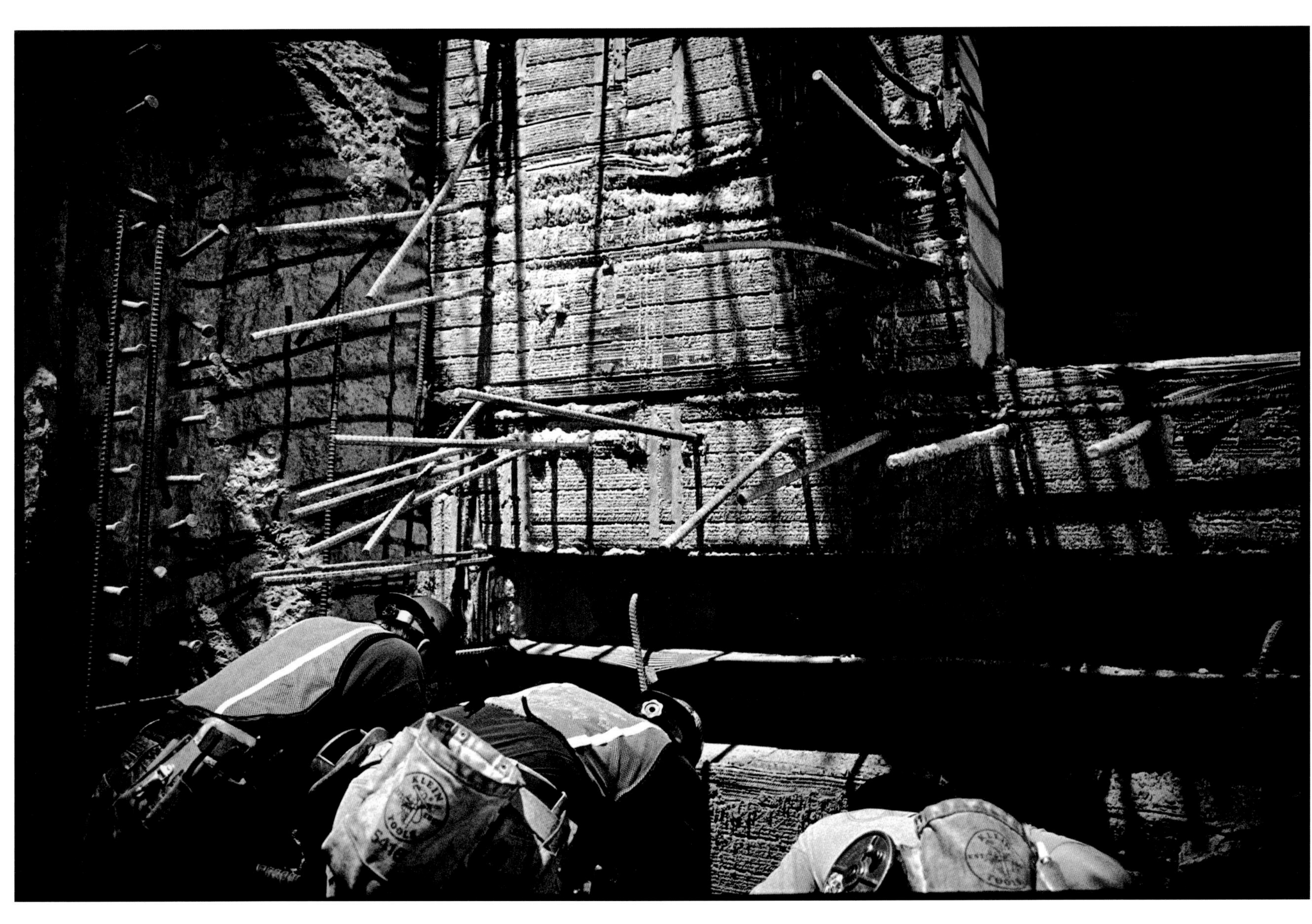

Tying rebar under
Causeway Street
2001

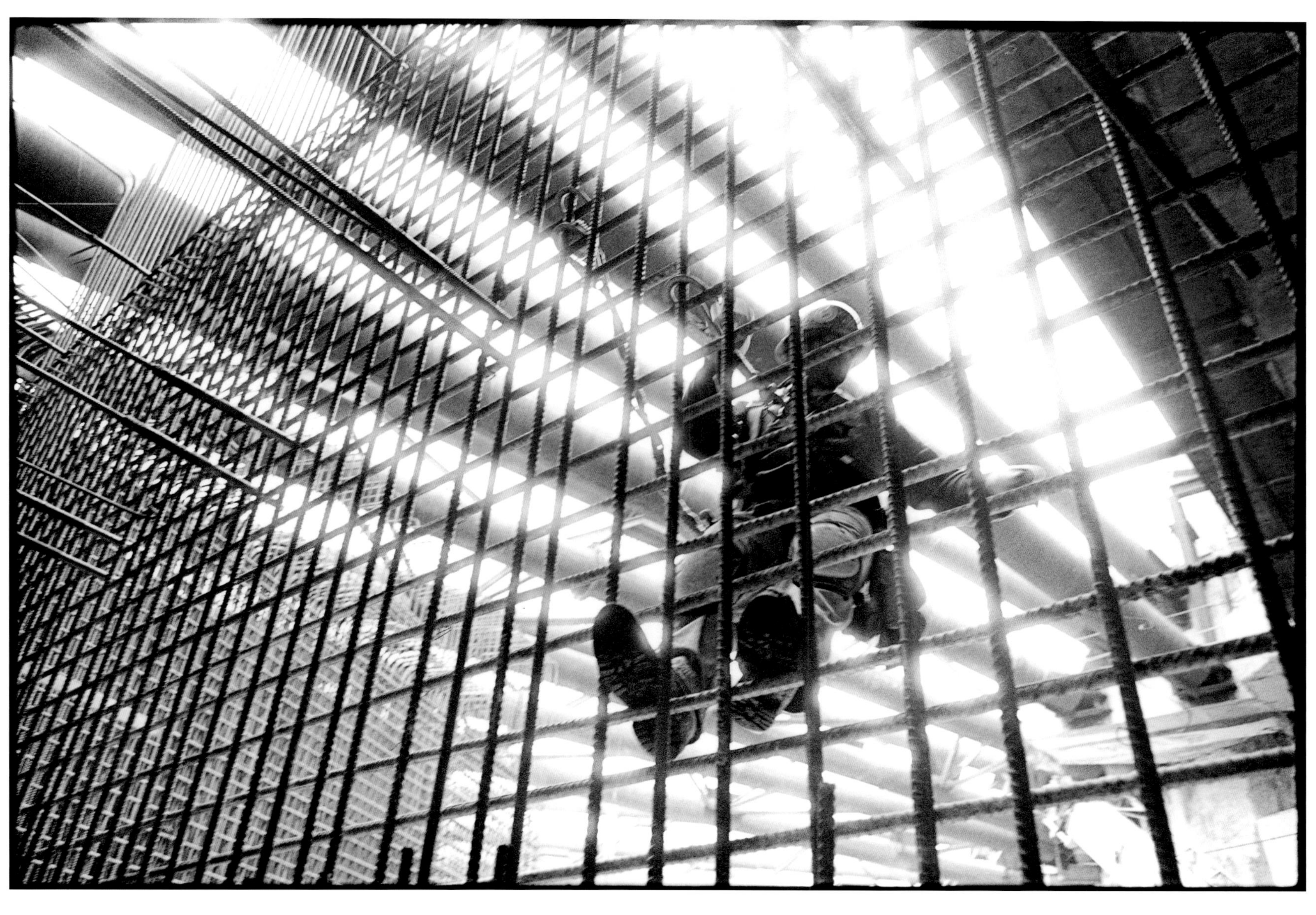

Rebar wall, Massachusetts
Turnpike interchange near
South Station
2000

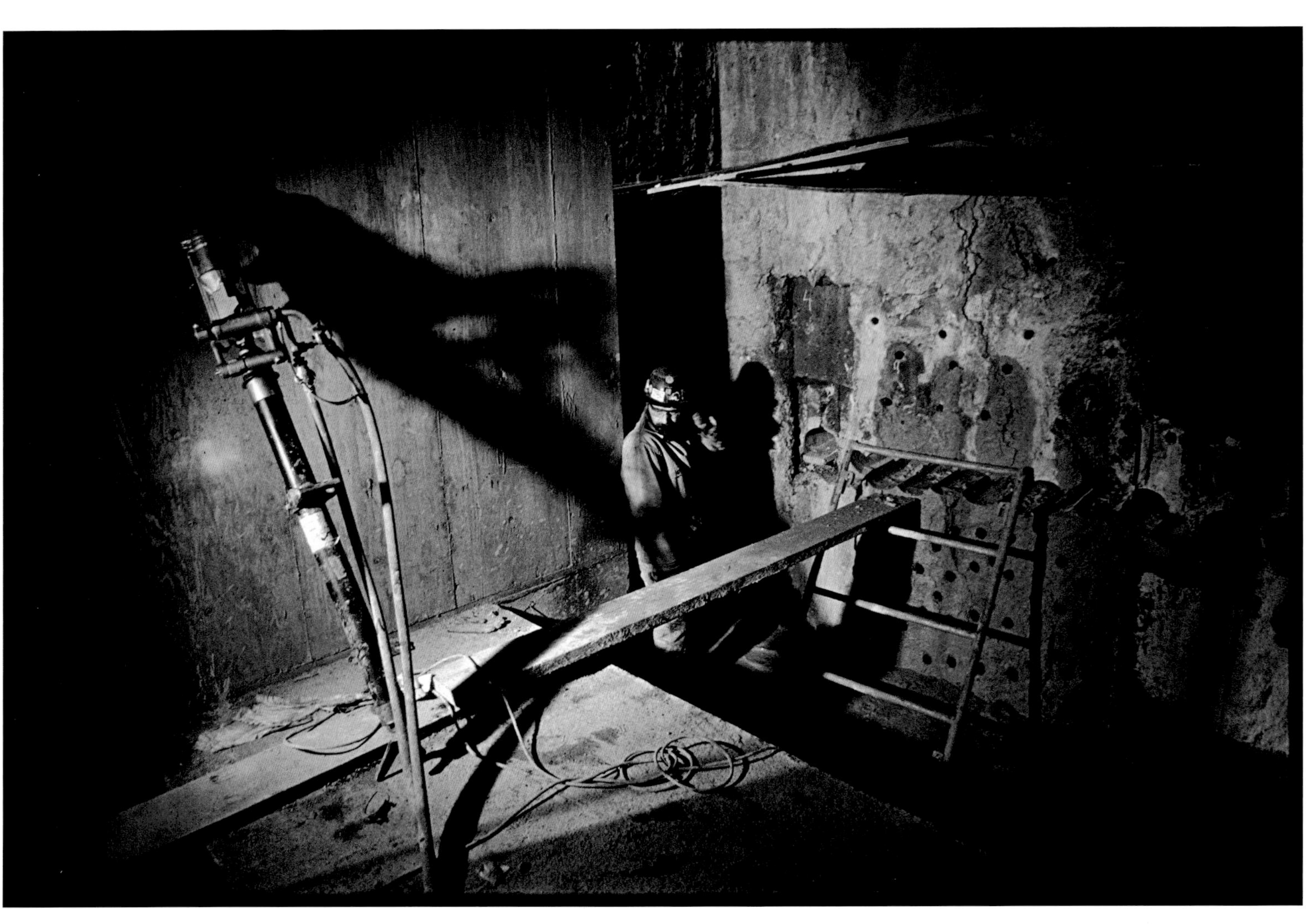

Tunnel worker,
near South Station
1999

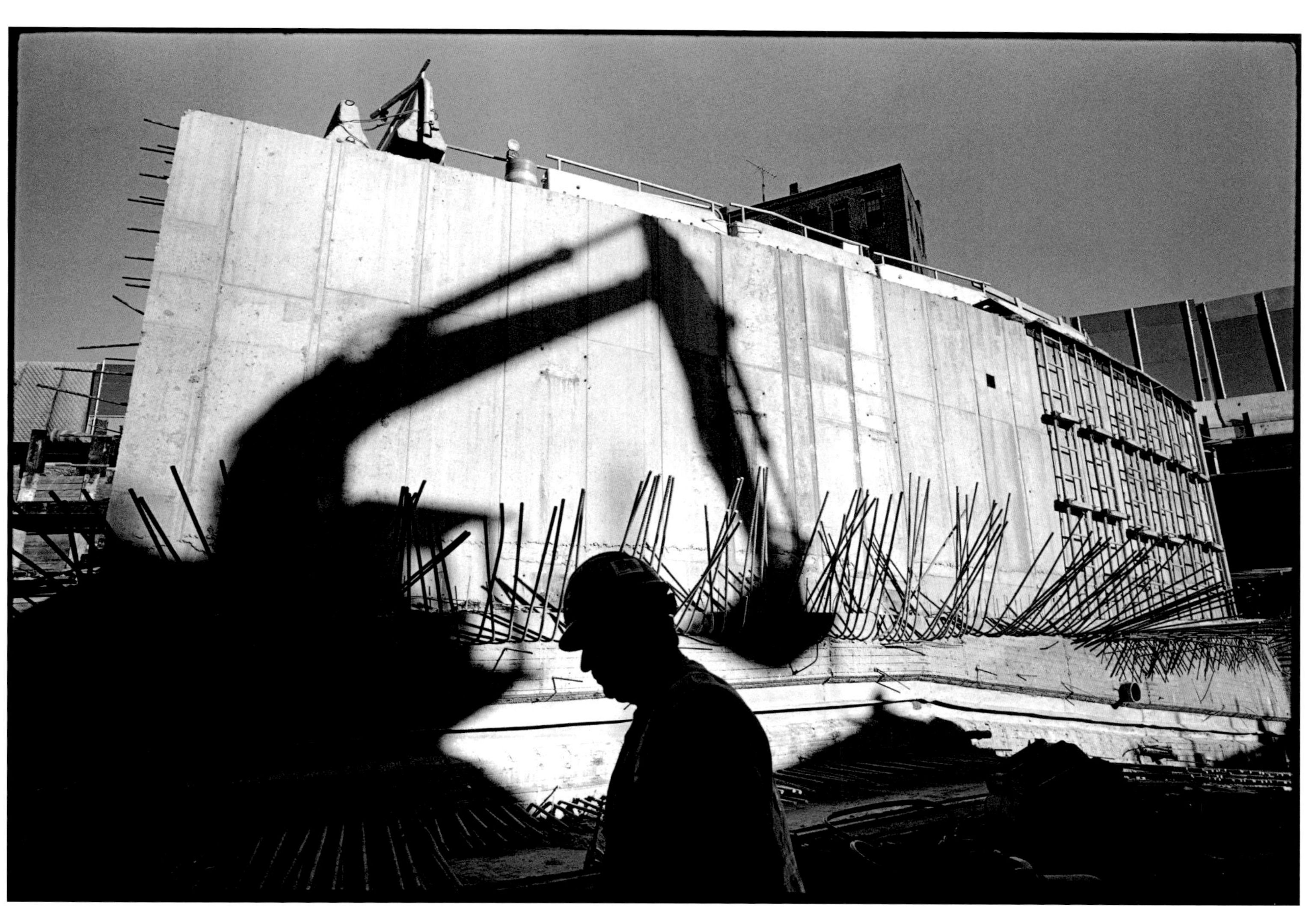

Tunnel wall,
North End
2001

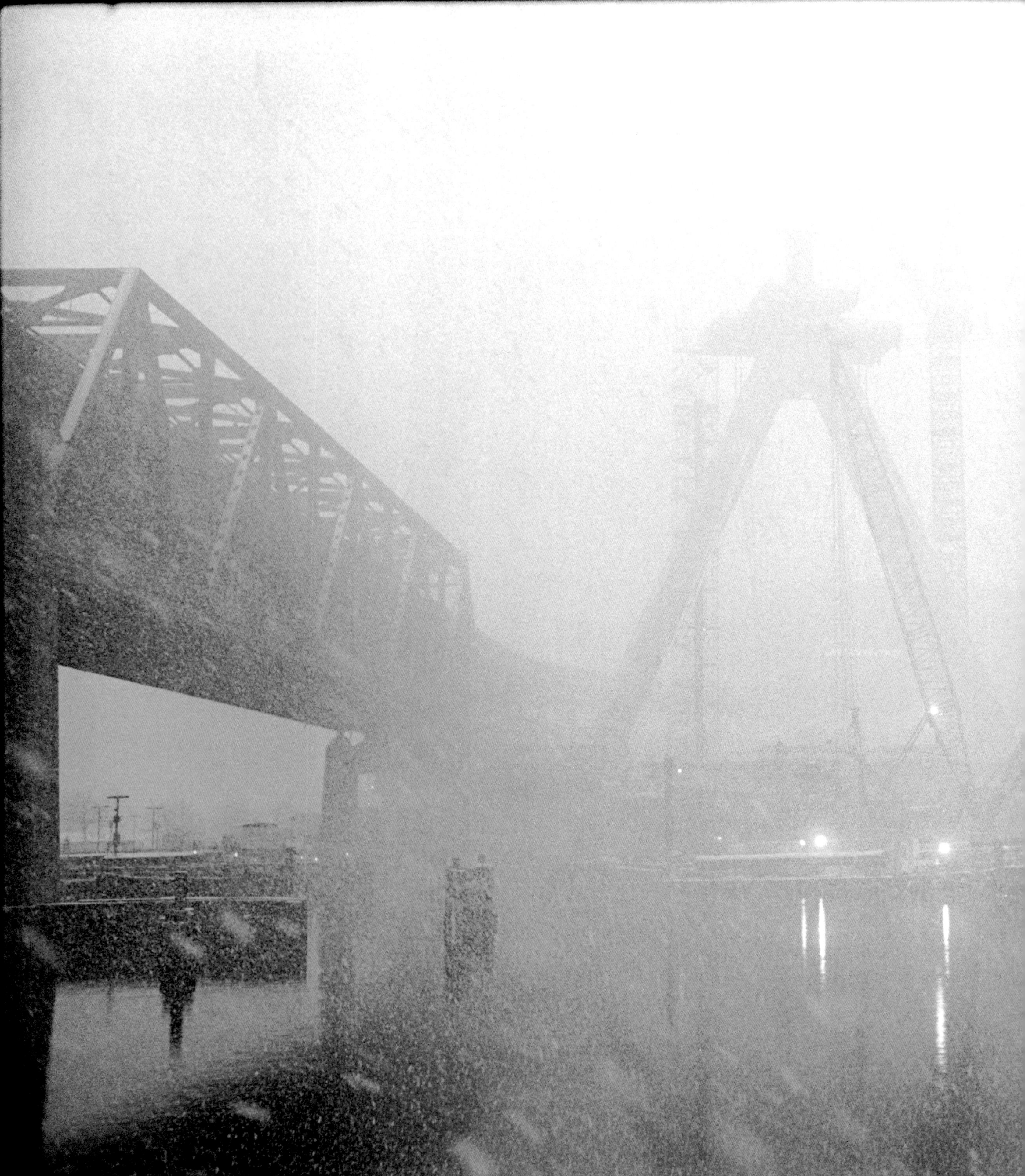

South tower of the
Zakim Bridge
winter 2000

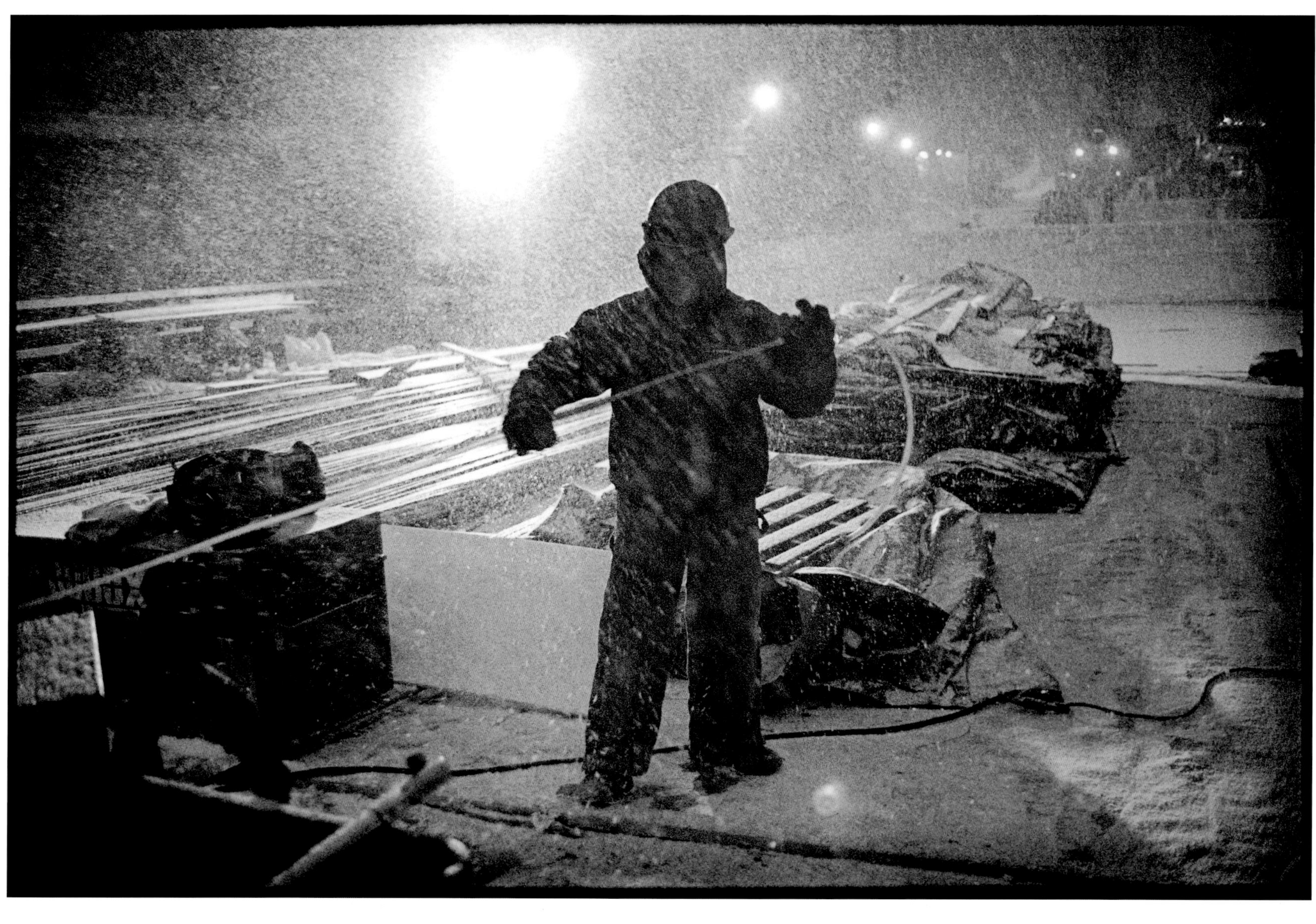

Predawn snow squall,
near High Street
2003

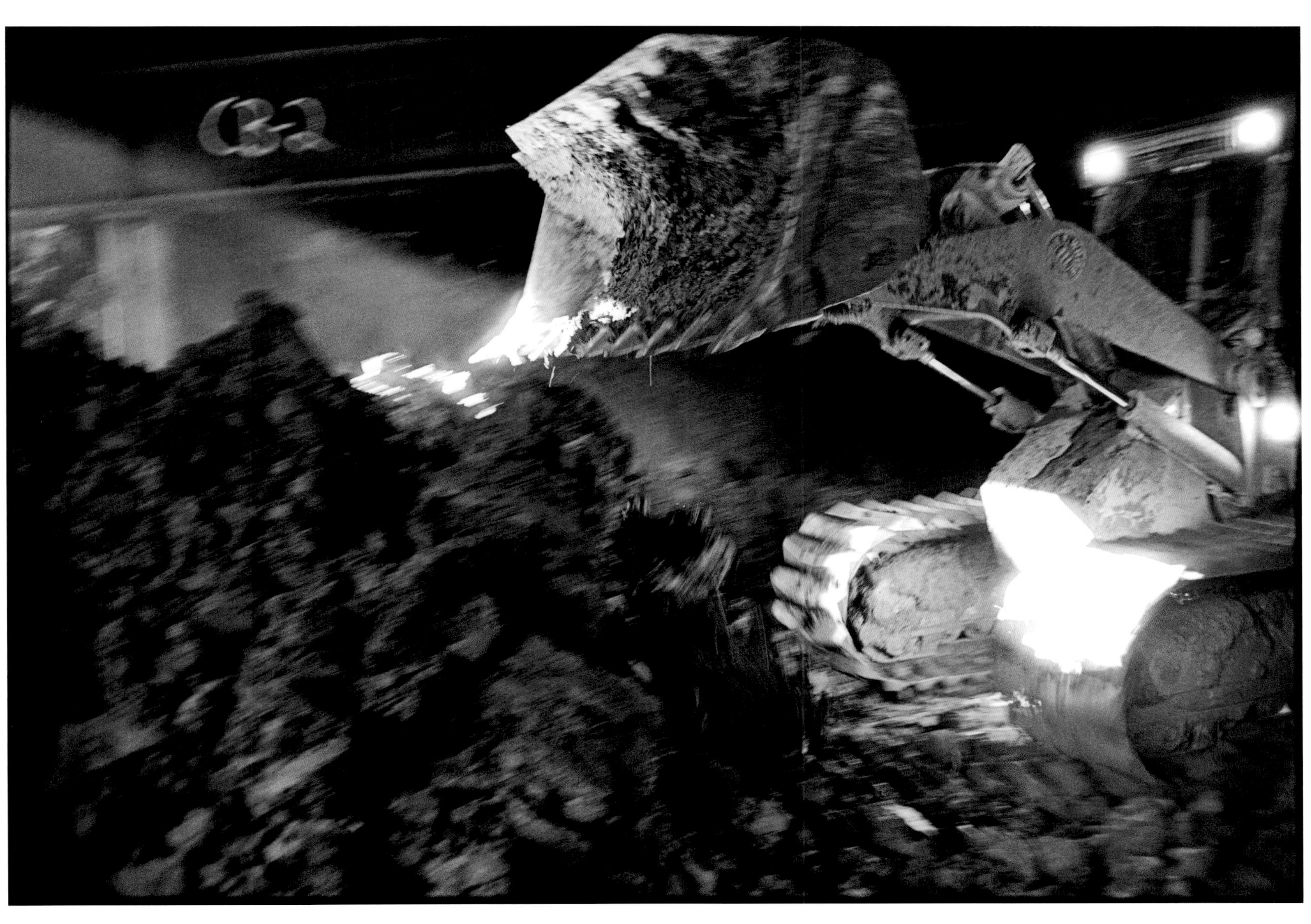

Bulldozer under Dock Square
2000

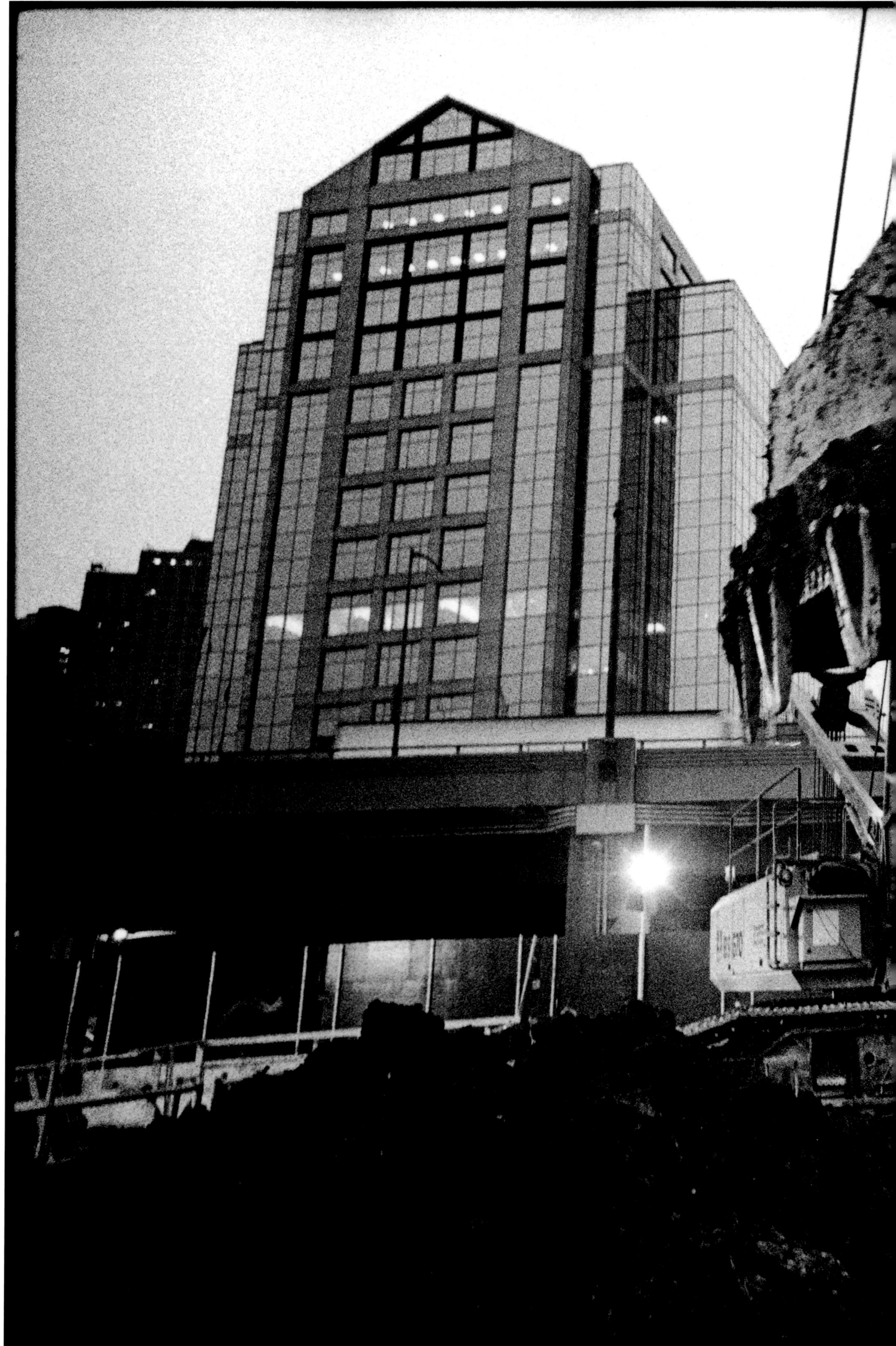

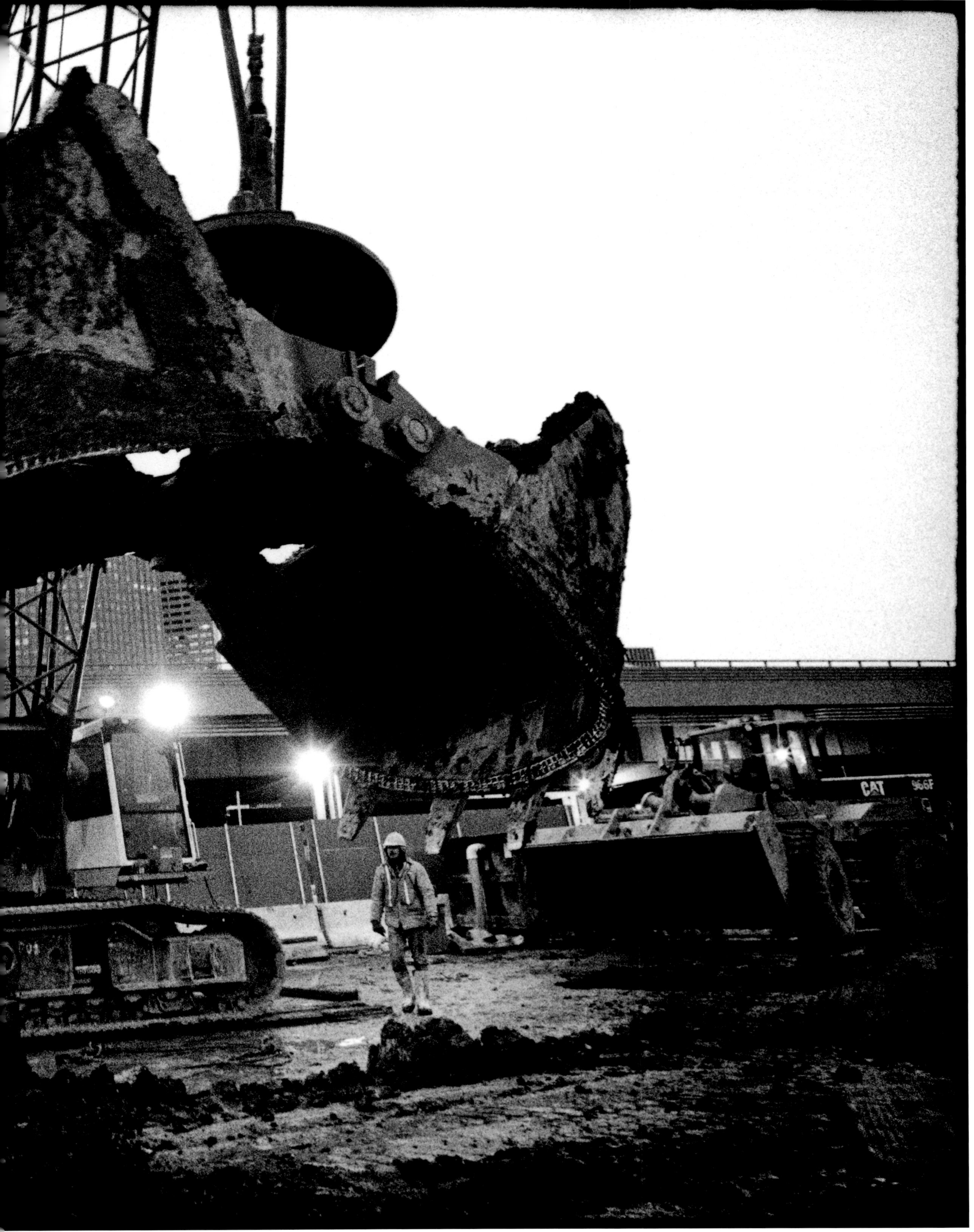
CAT 966F

◄ Digging at dusk,
Atlantic Avenue
1998

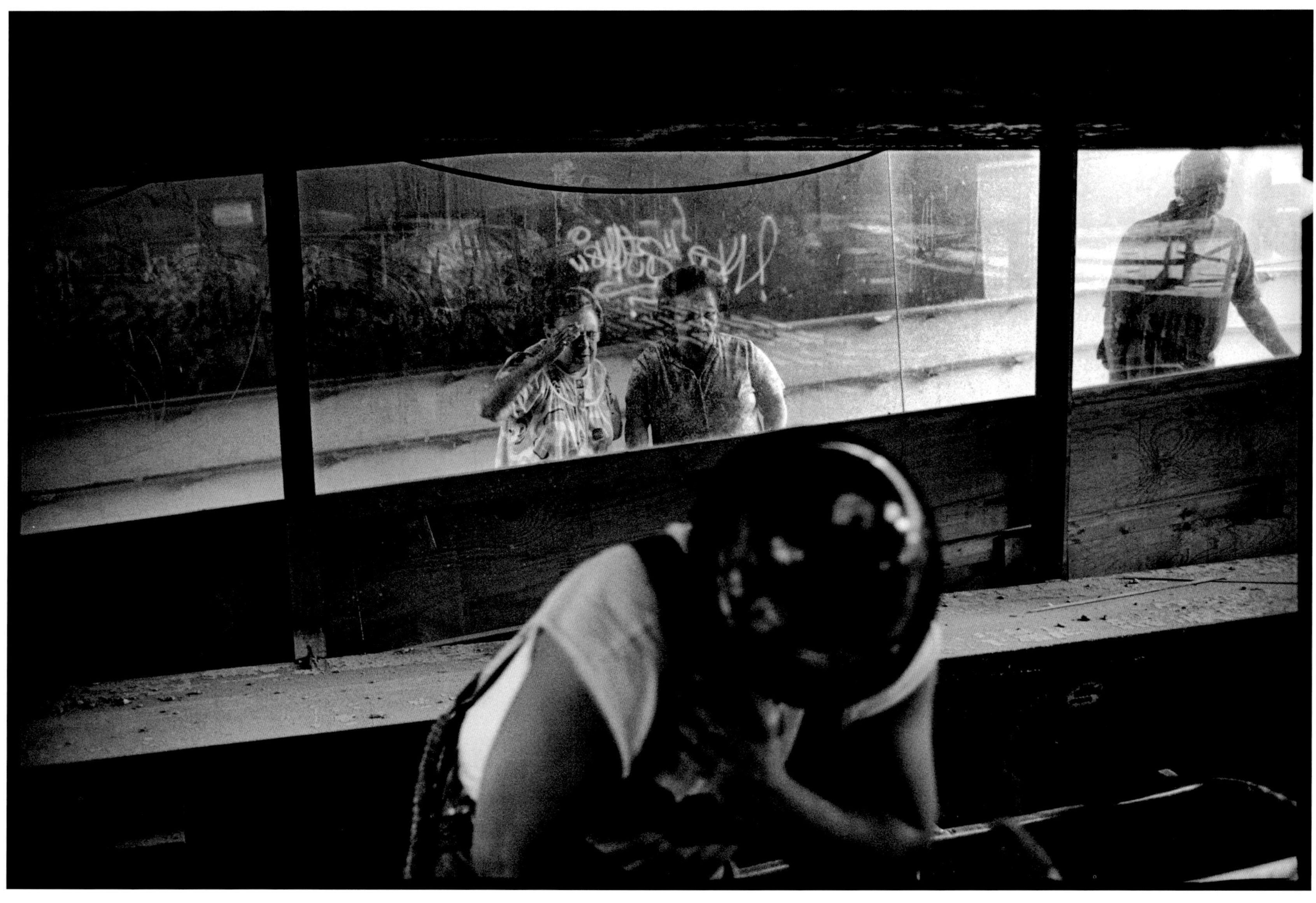

Onlookers, the Freedom Trail
at the North End
2002

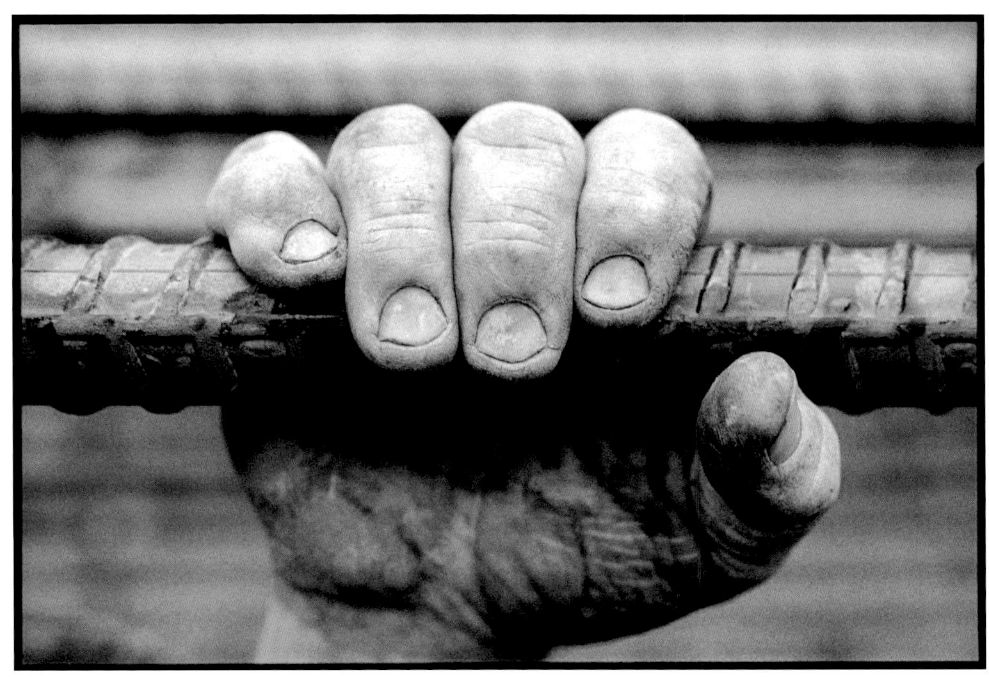

Near the Silver Line
1999

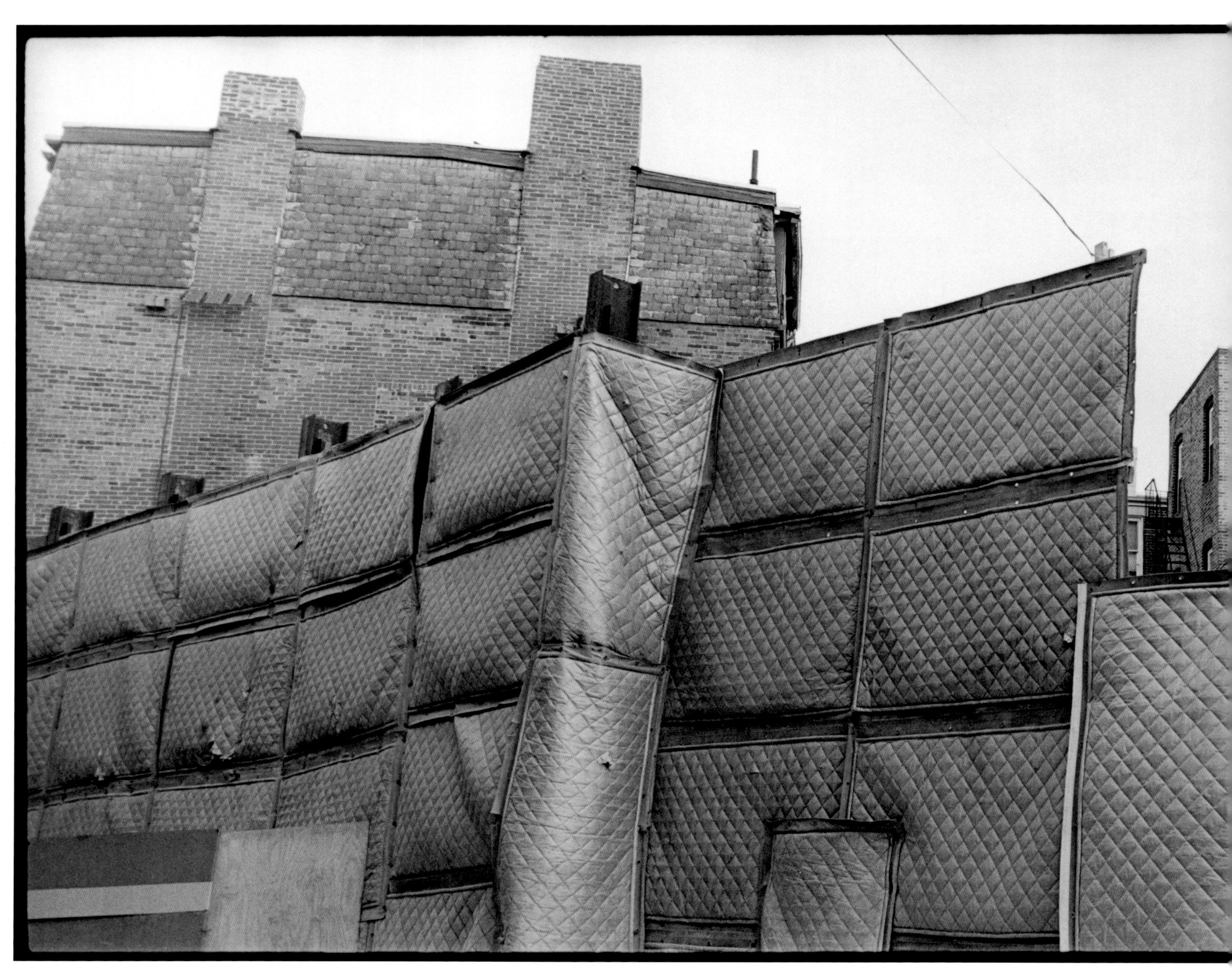

Noise abatement, North End at
North Washington Street
2000

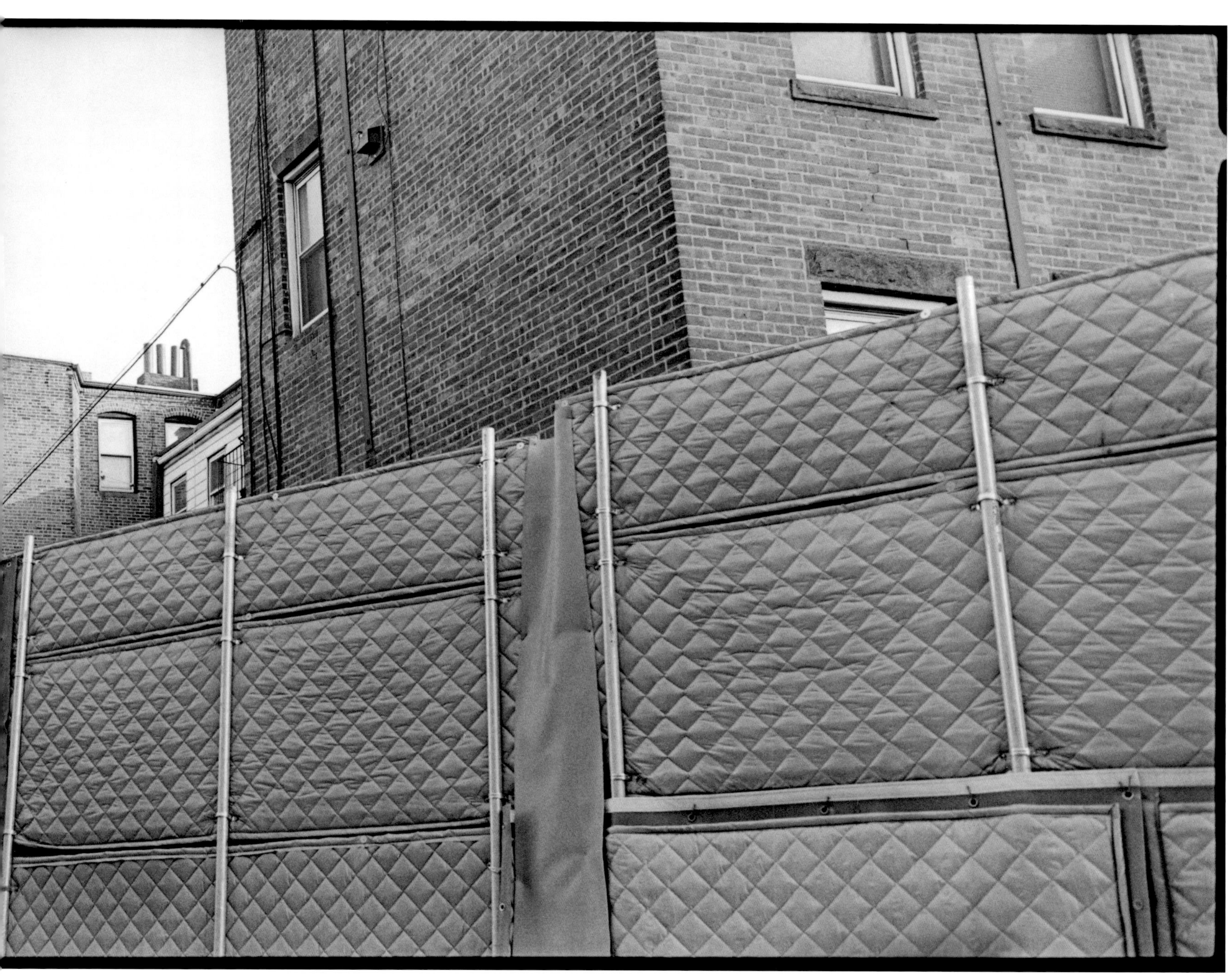

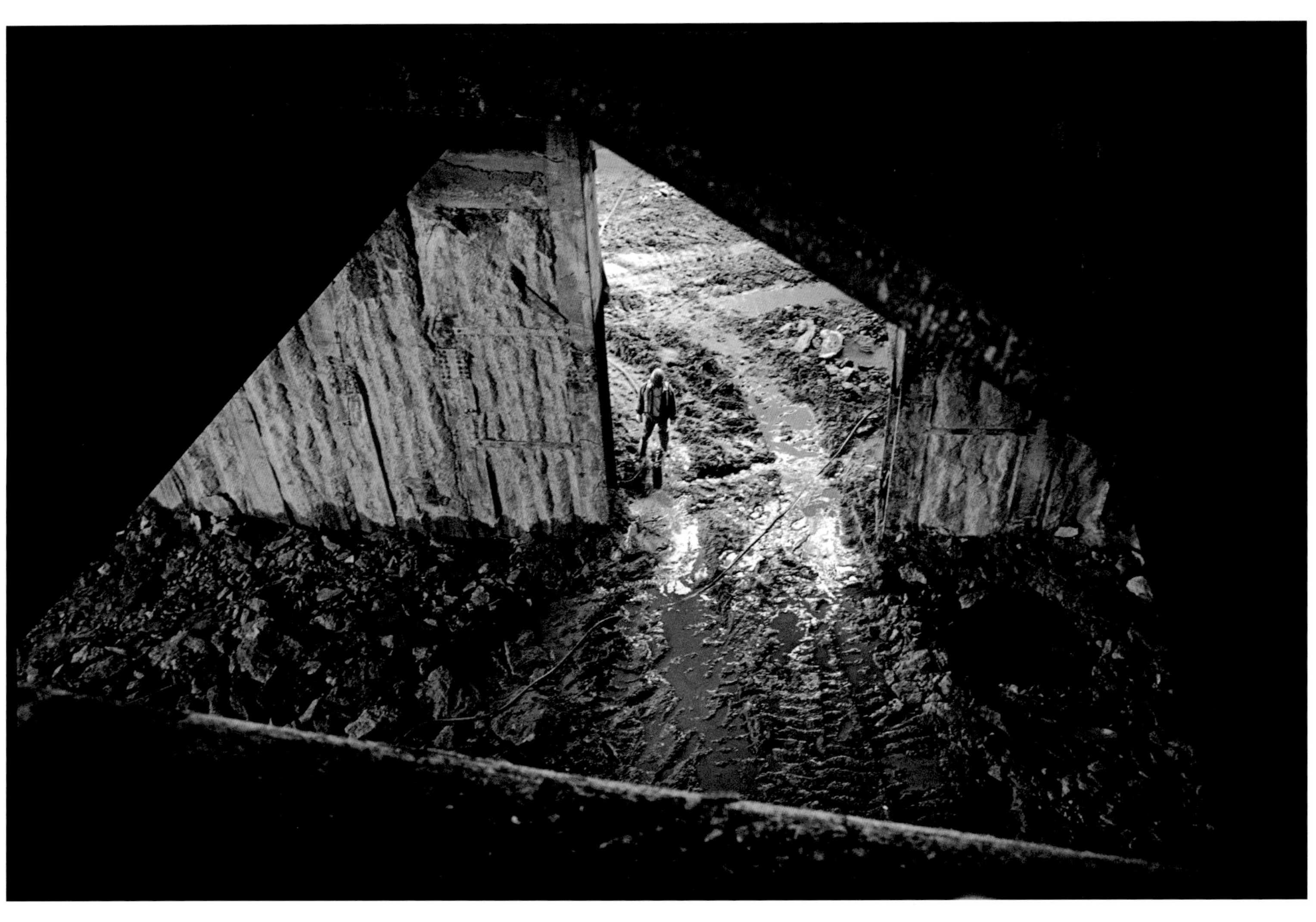

Under Dock Square
2000

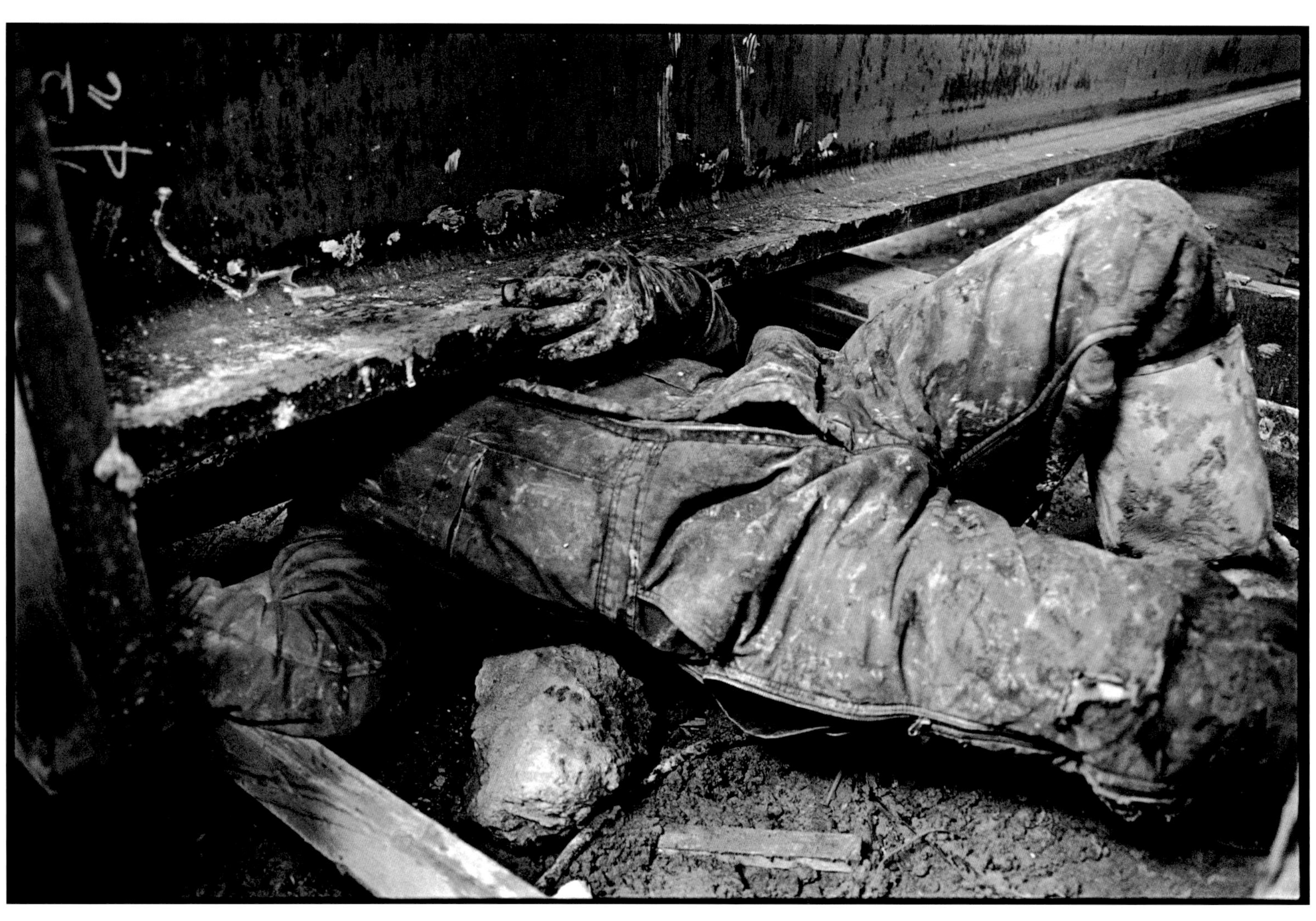

Under a beam,
Broad Street
2000

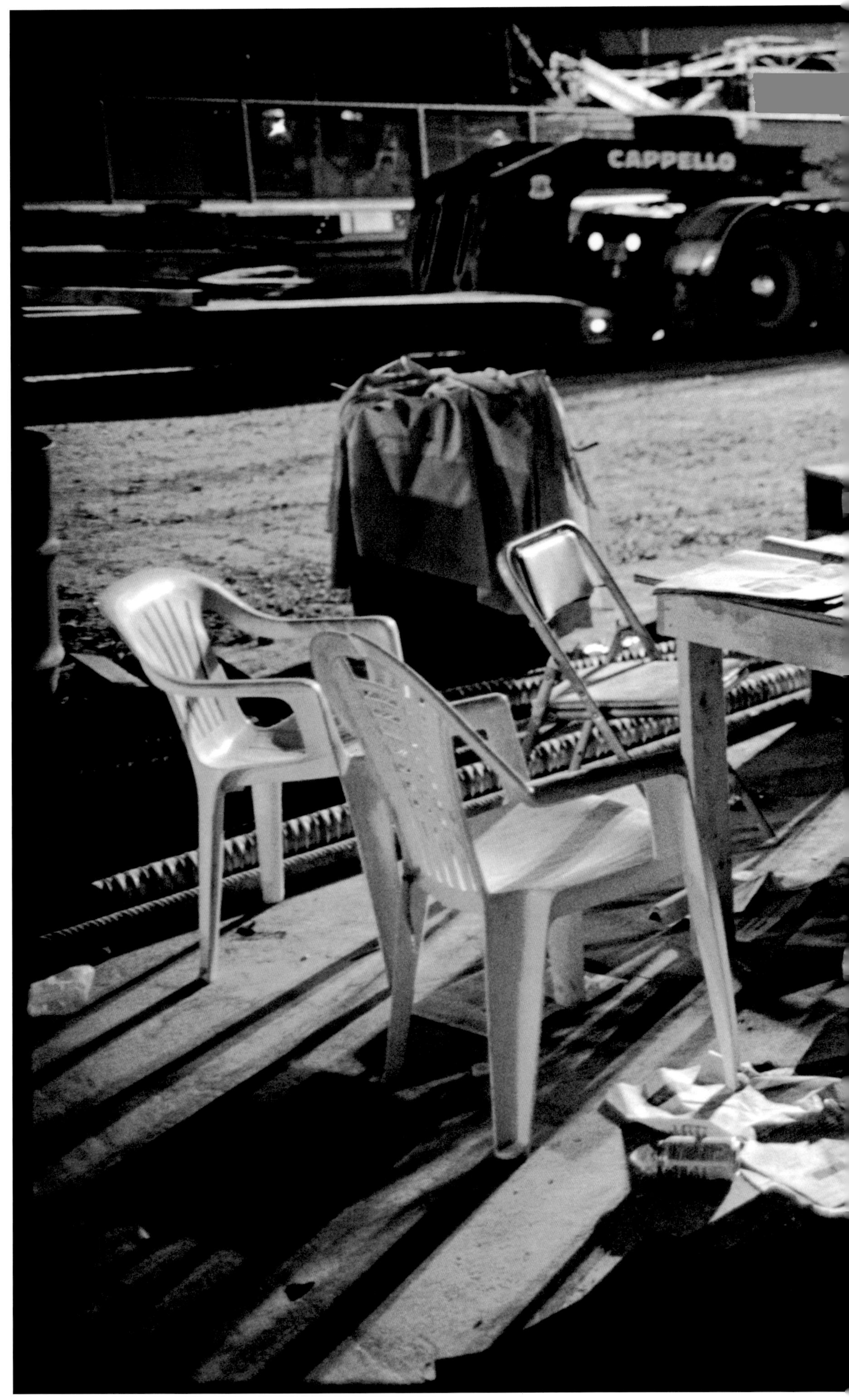

Break table, 1:00 a.m.,
under Leverett Connector
summer 2000

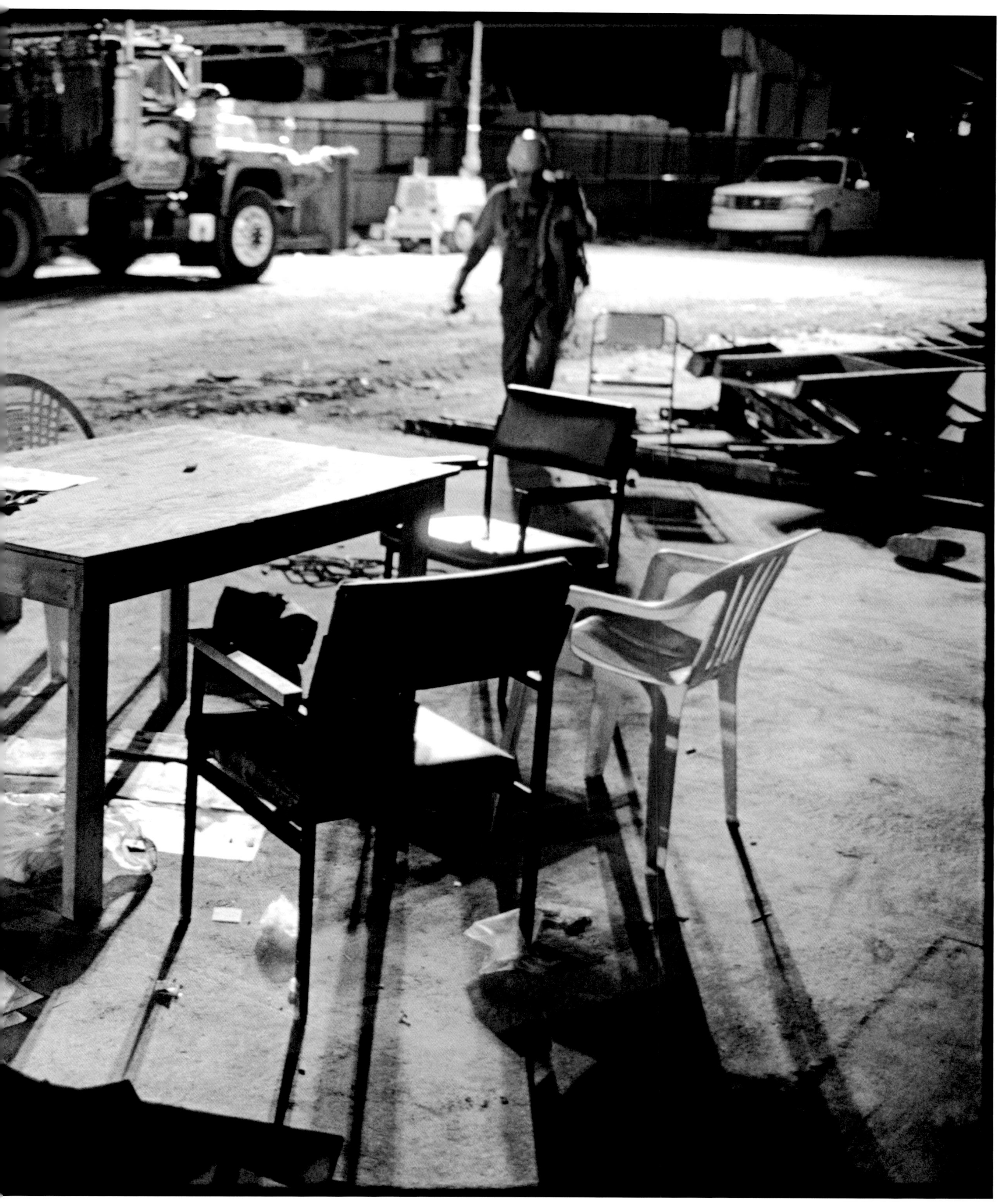

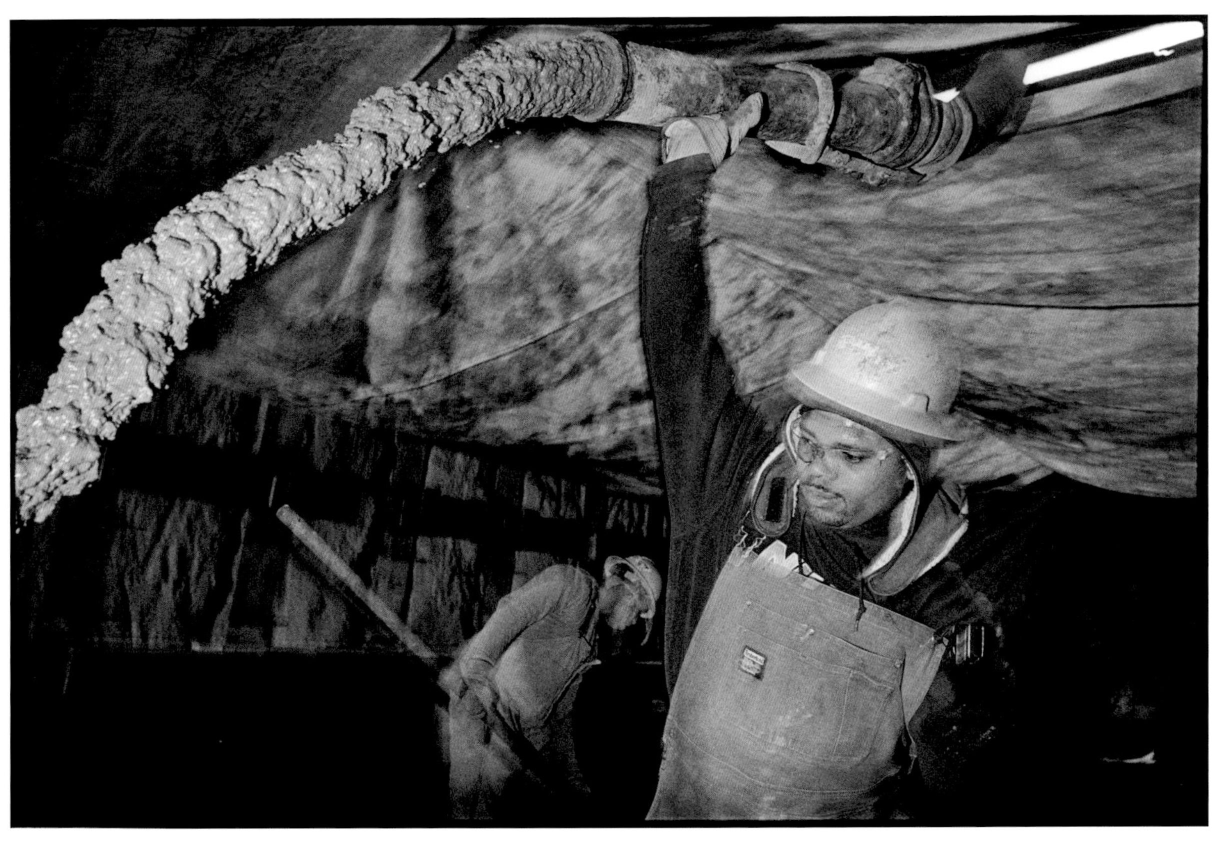

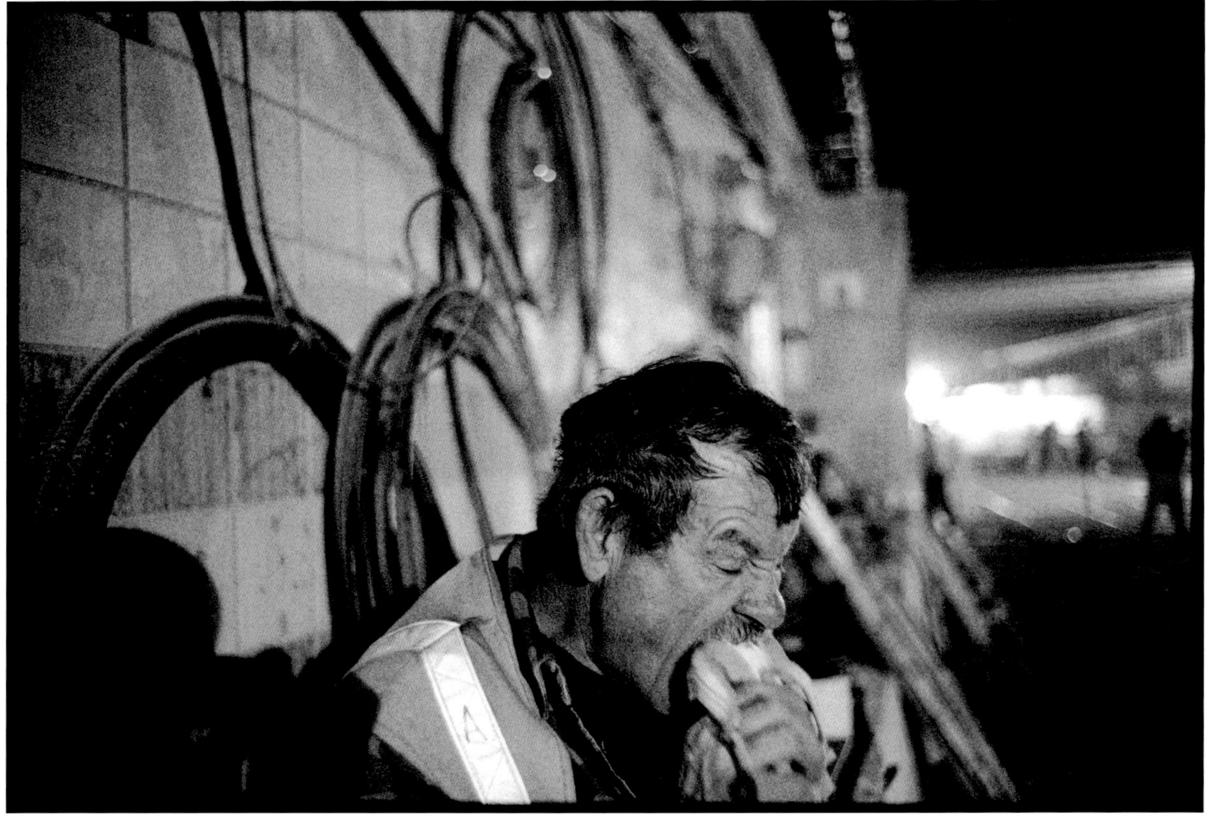

Laborer and concrete hose, near High Street, 2004

Break, Dewey Square Tunnel section, 2004

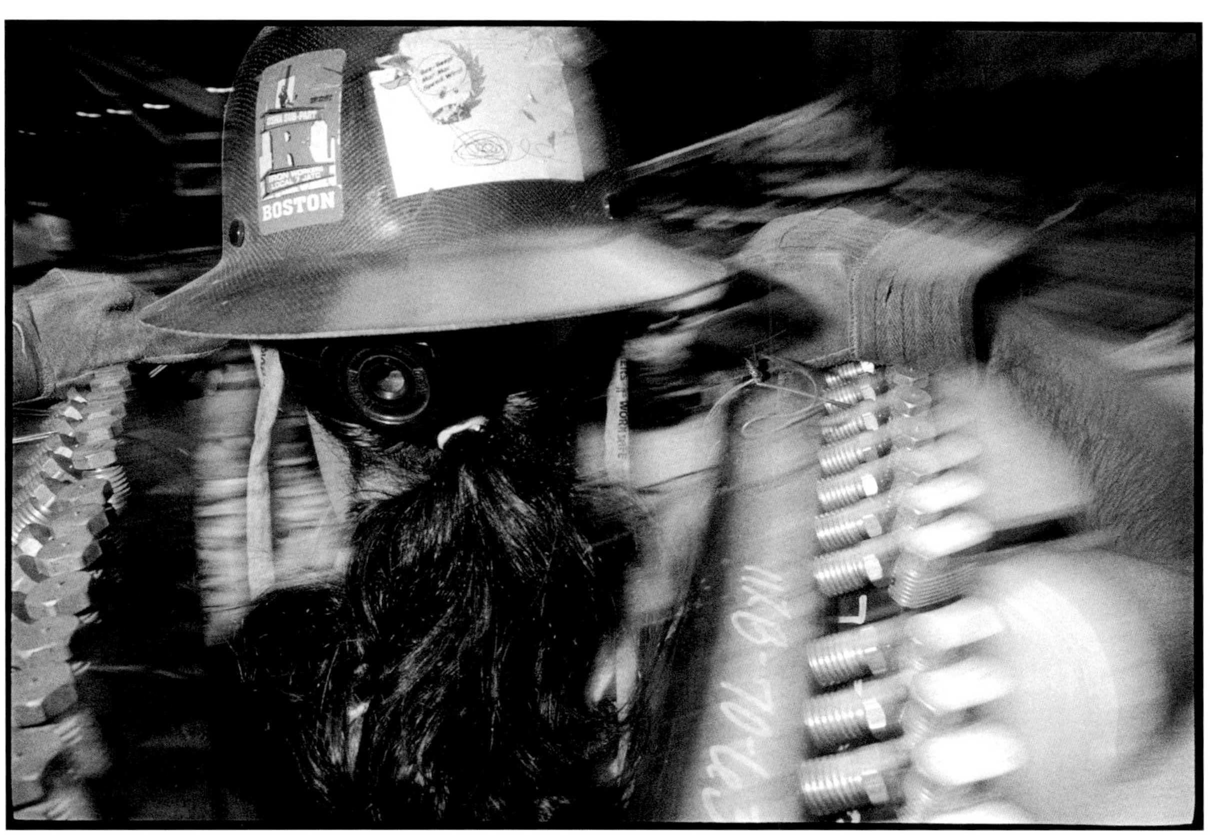

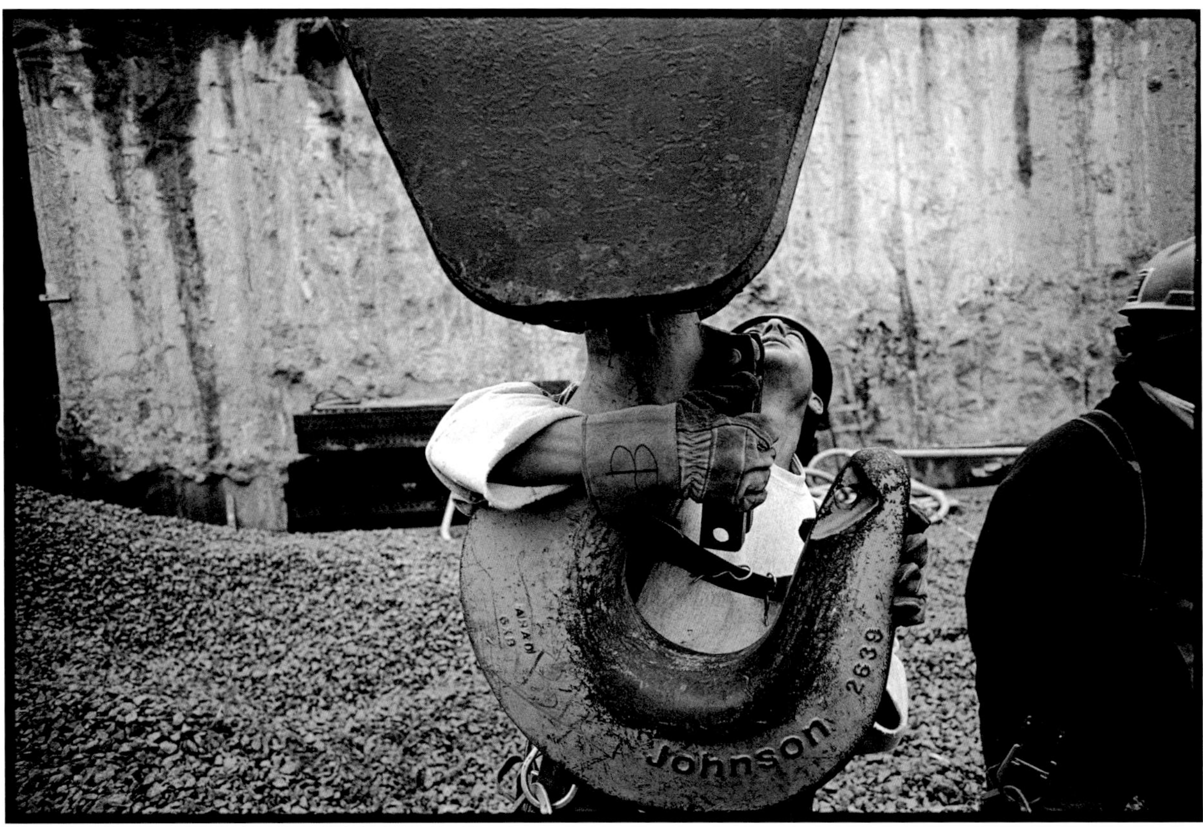

Rebar splice sleeves, near High Street, 2003

Johnson block, south of South Station, 2001

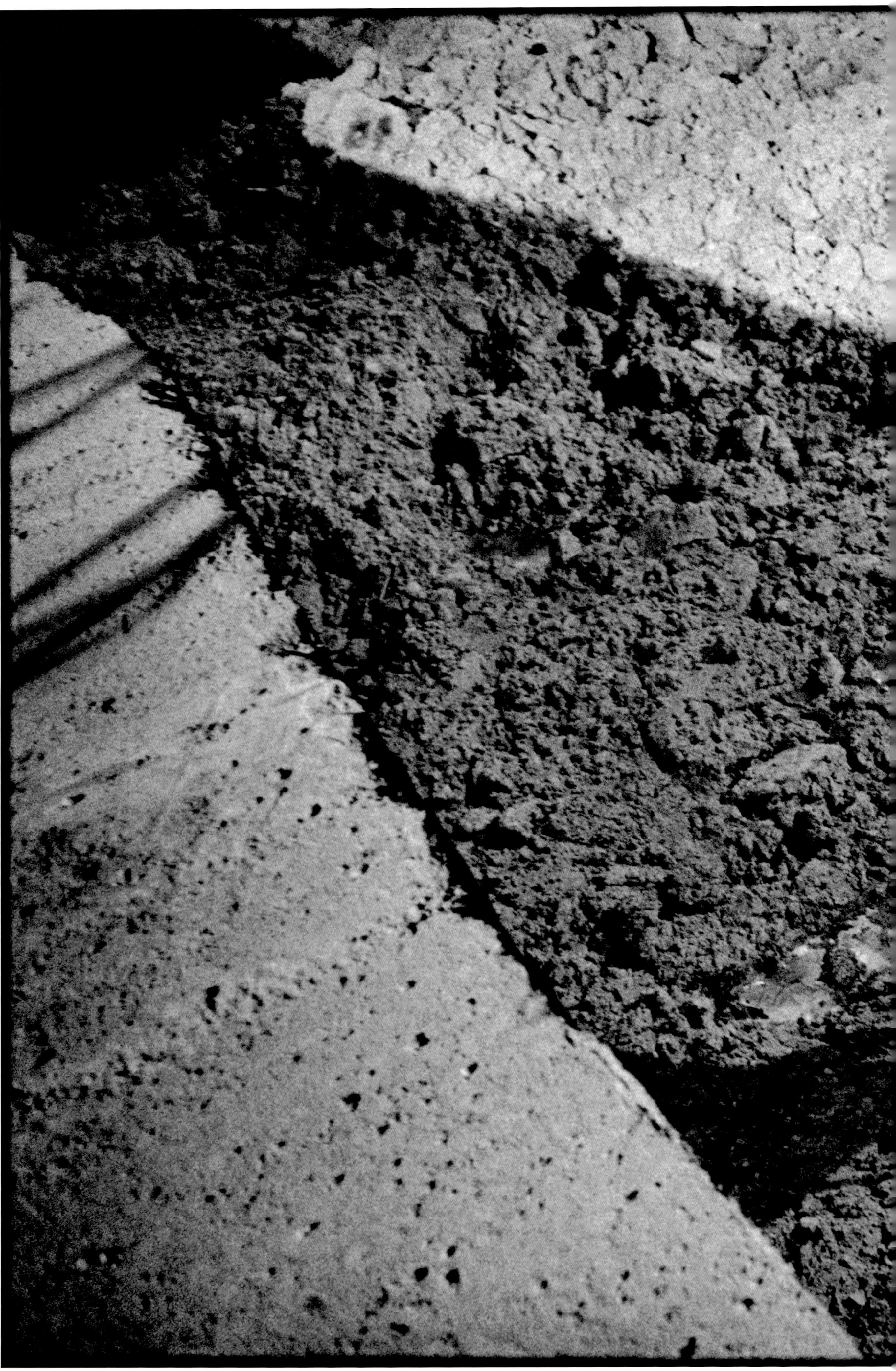

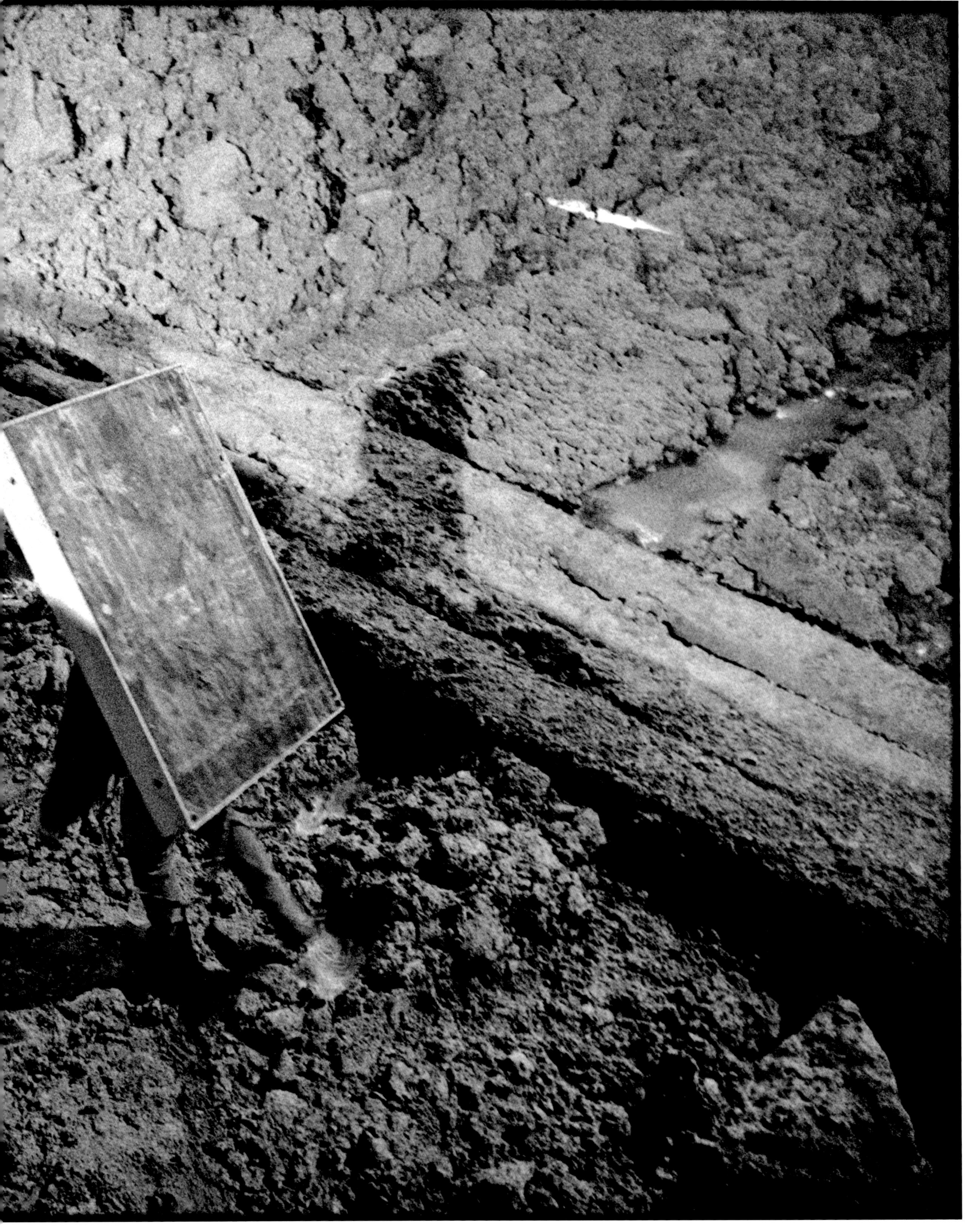

◄ Carrying a concrete form through mud,
under Causeway Street
2001

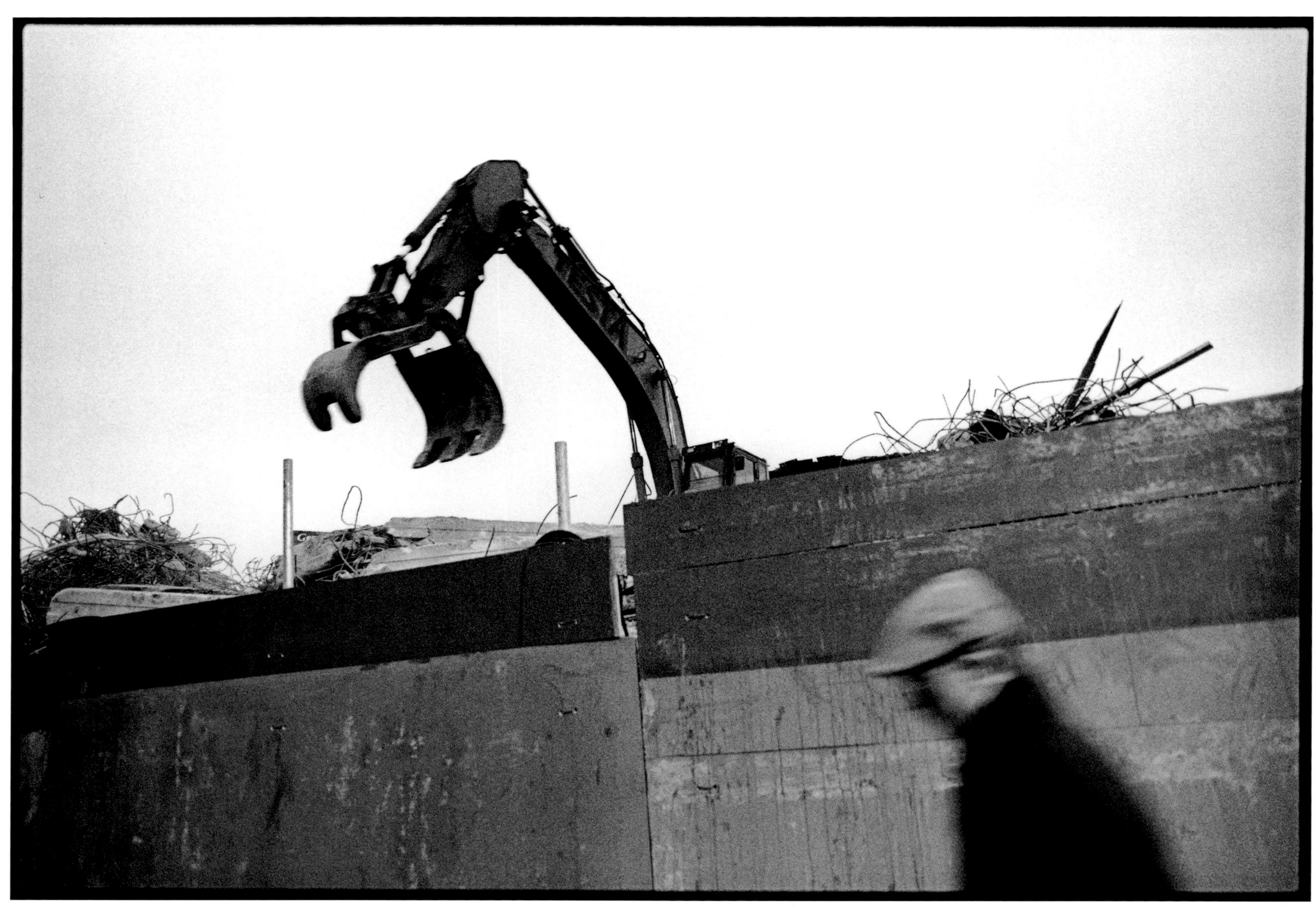

Demolition, Freedom Trail
at Haymarket
2004

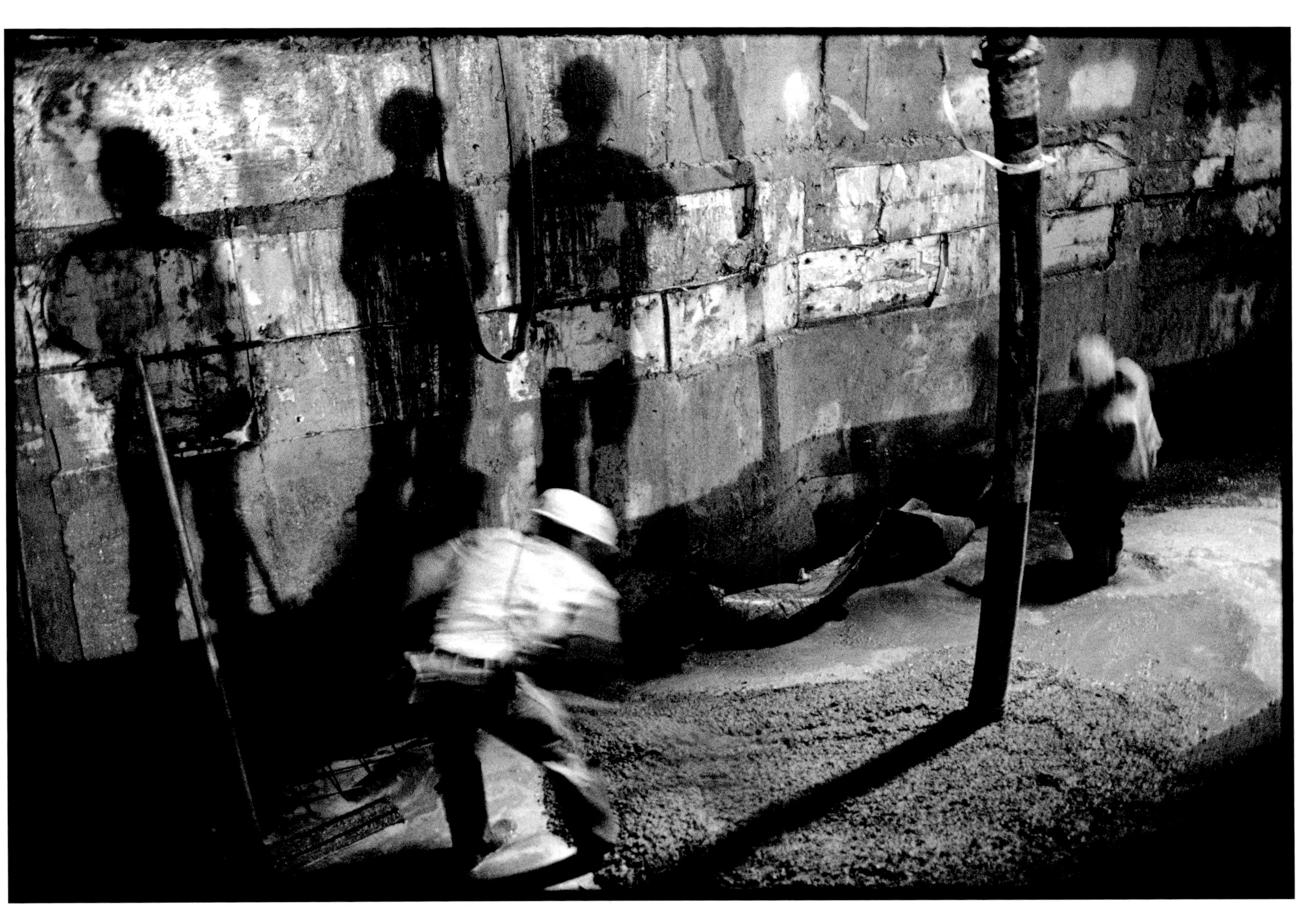

Pouring concrete under
Summer Street
2003

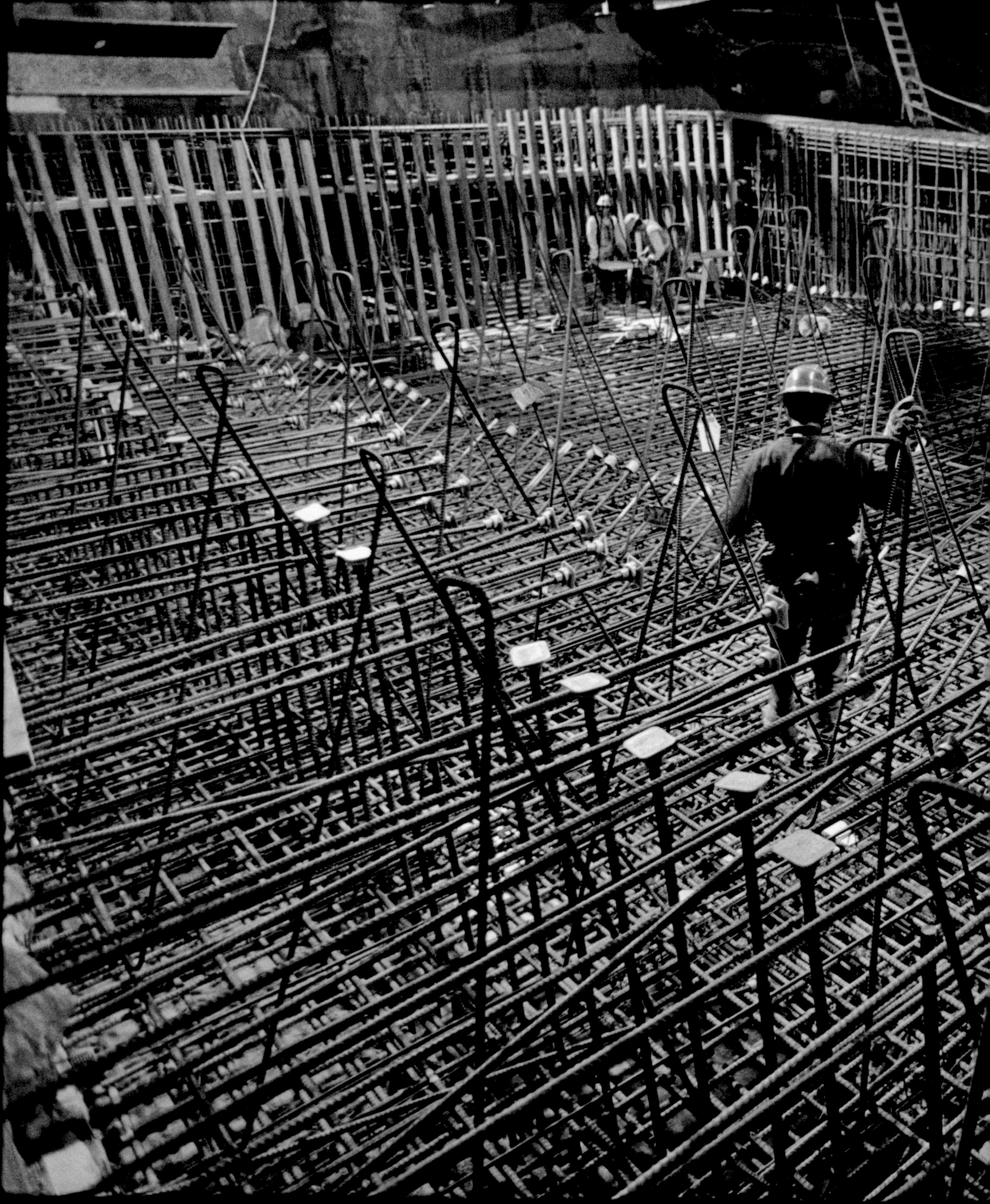

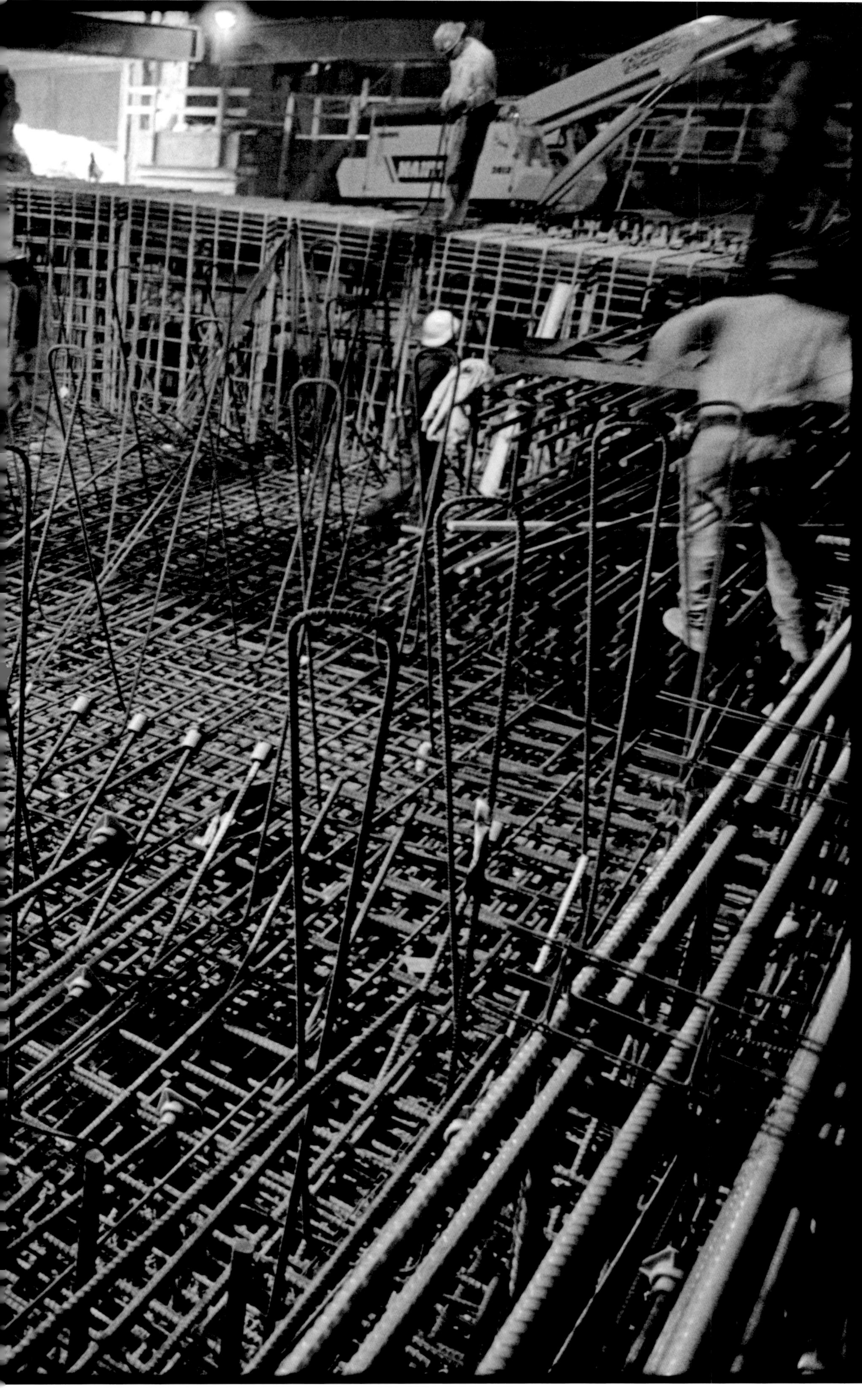

Rebar next to Blue Line
at State Street
1999

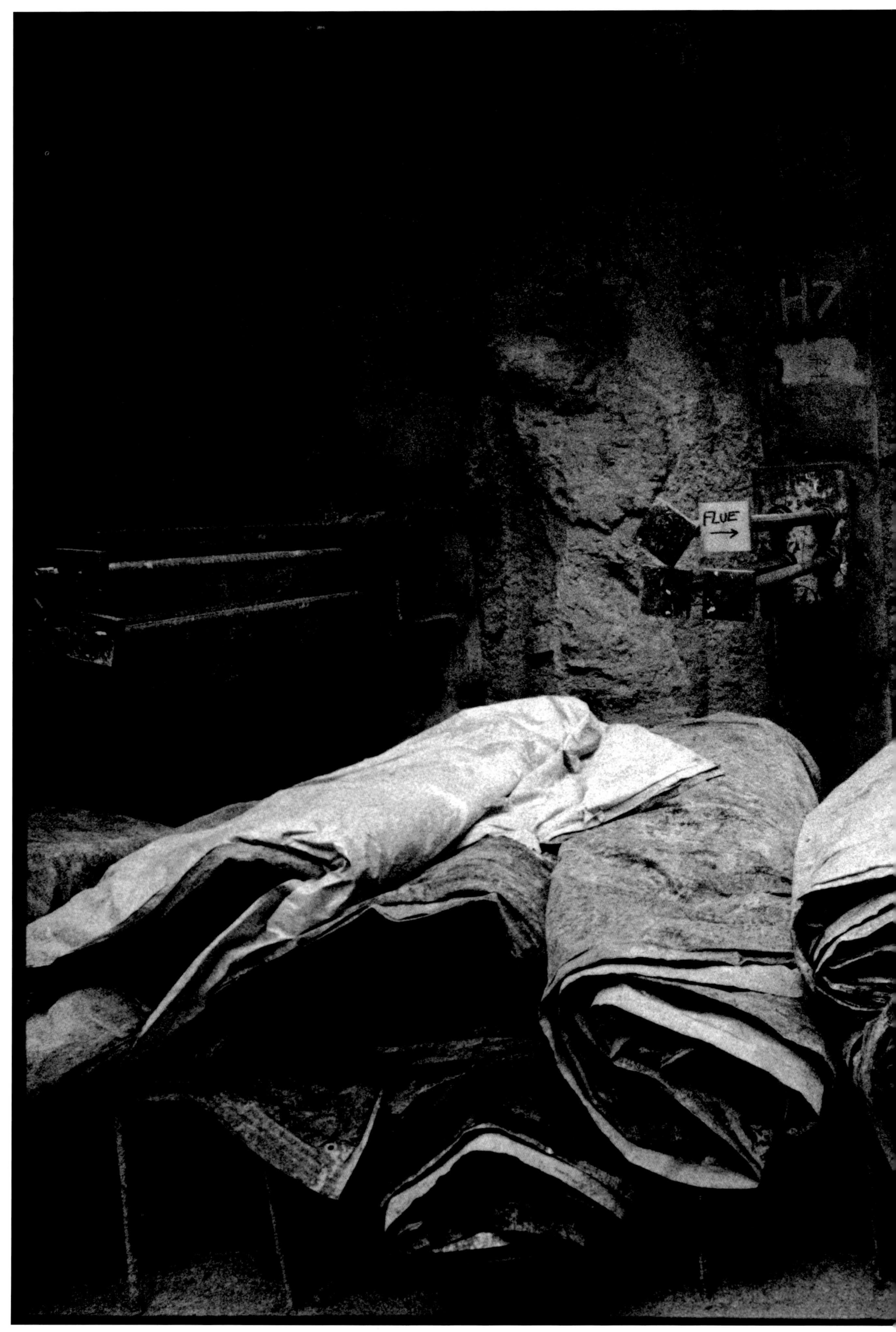

Tarps for keeping concrete
warm, near High Street
winter 2004

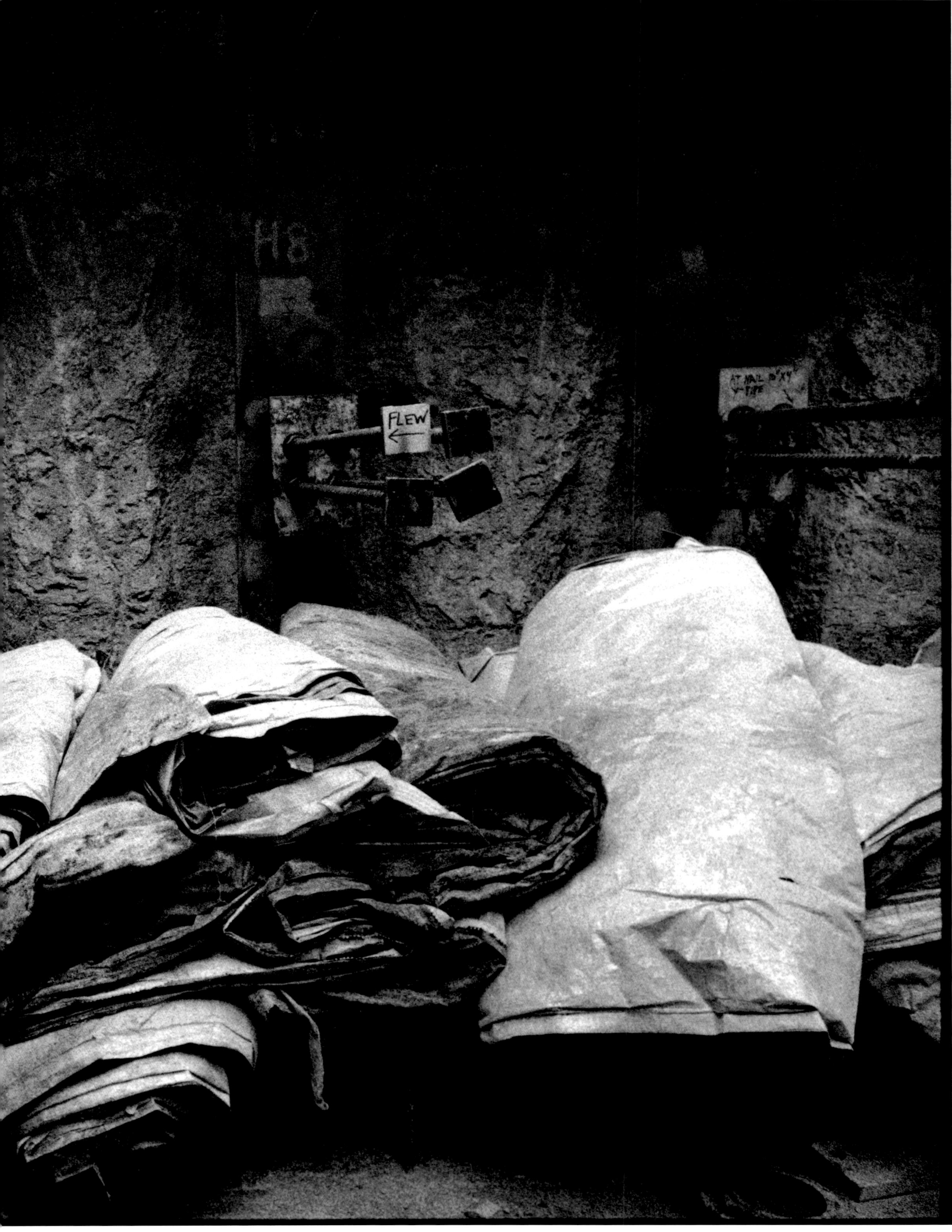
H8
FLEW

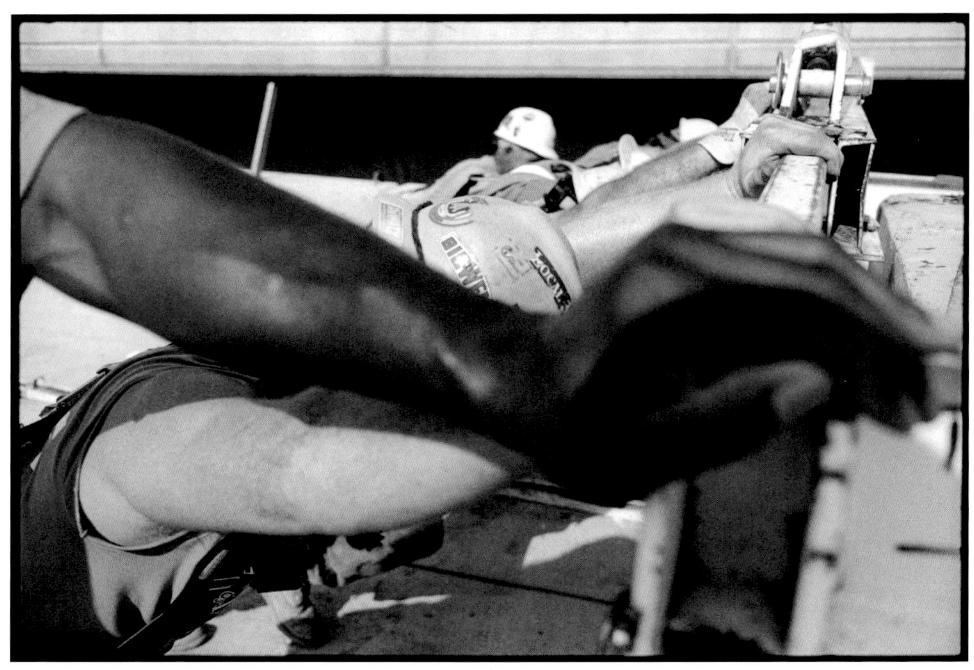

Pushing form into place,
I-93 loop ramp
2001

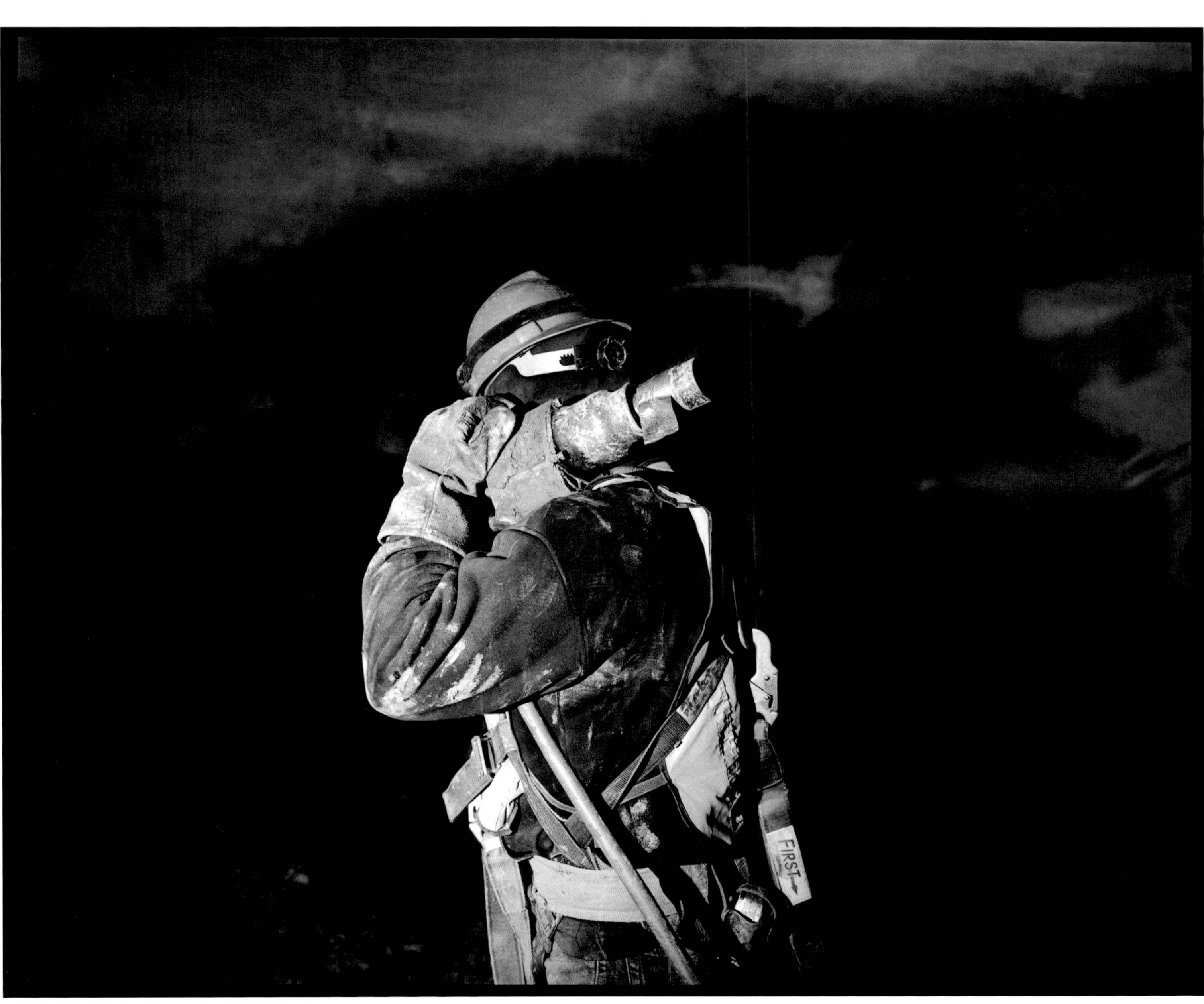

Pile driver with tool, under
North Washington Street
2000

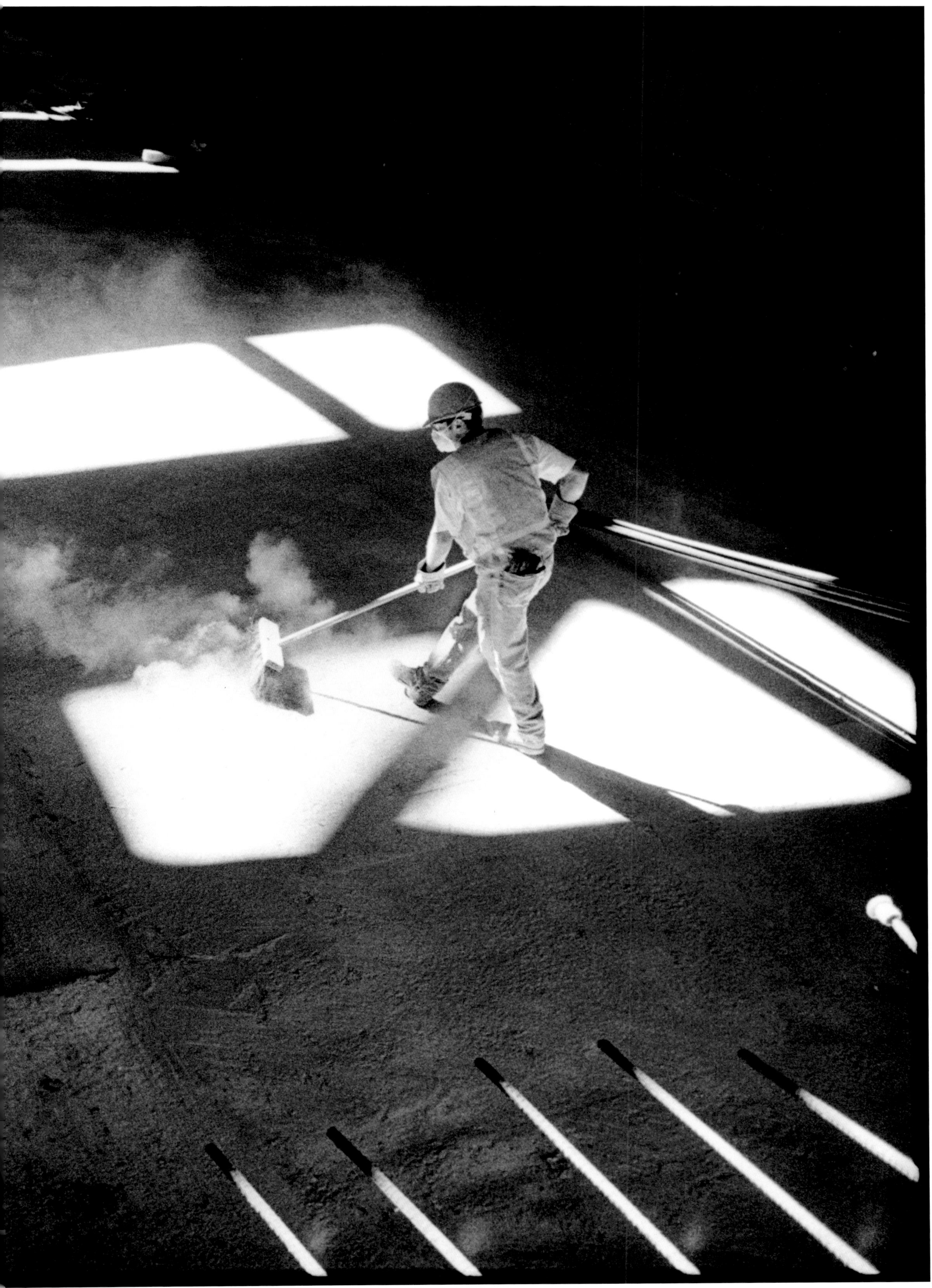

◀ Sweeping, near Dock Square
2001

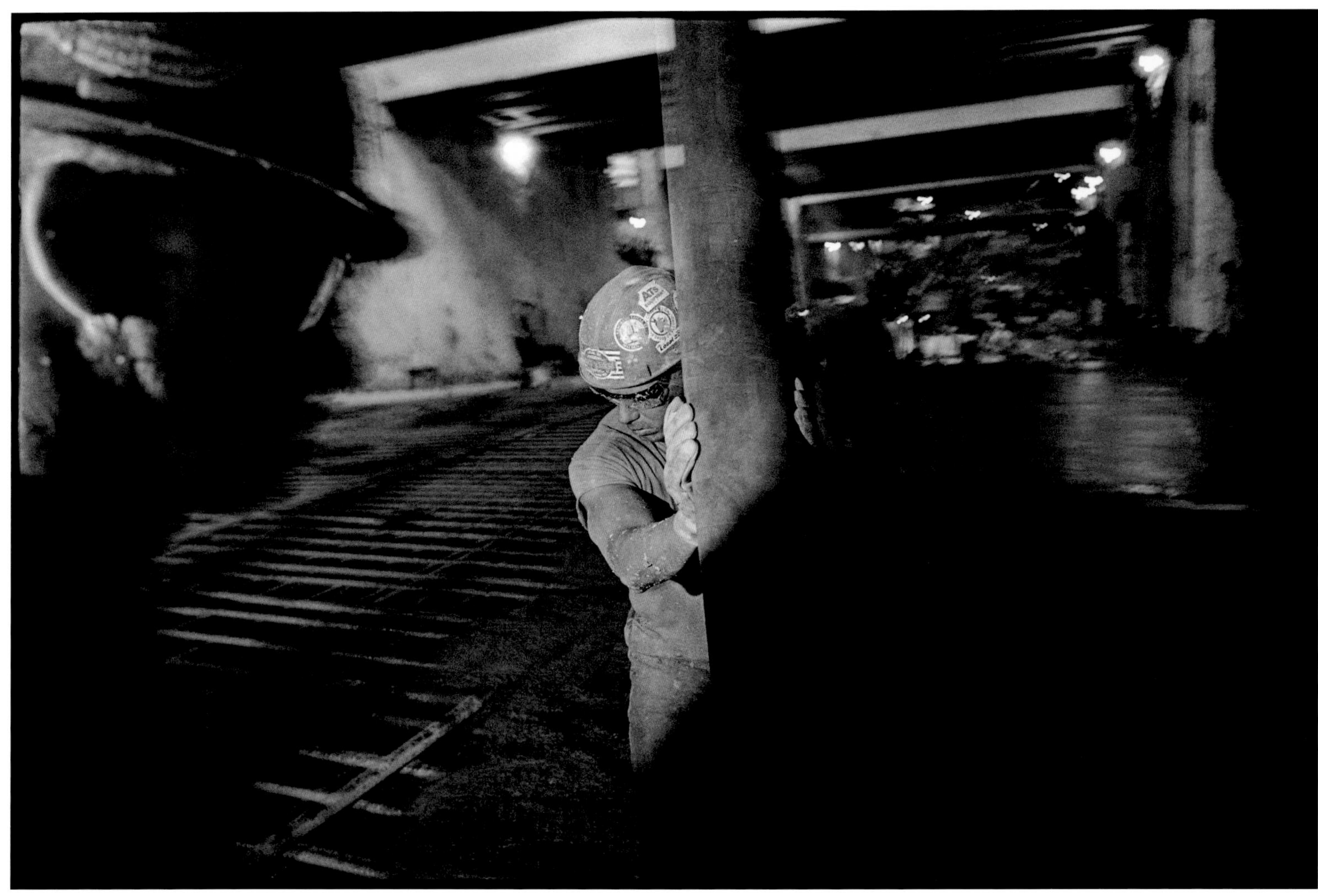

Pouring concrete under
North Washington Street
2001

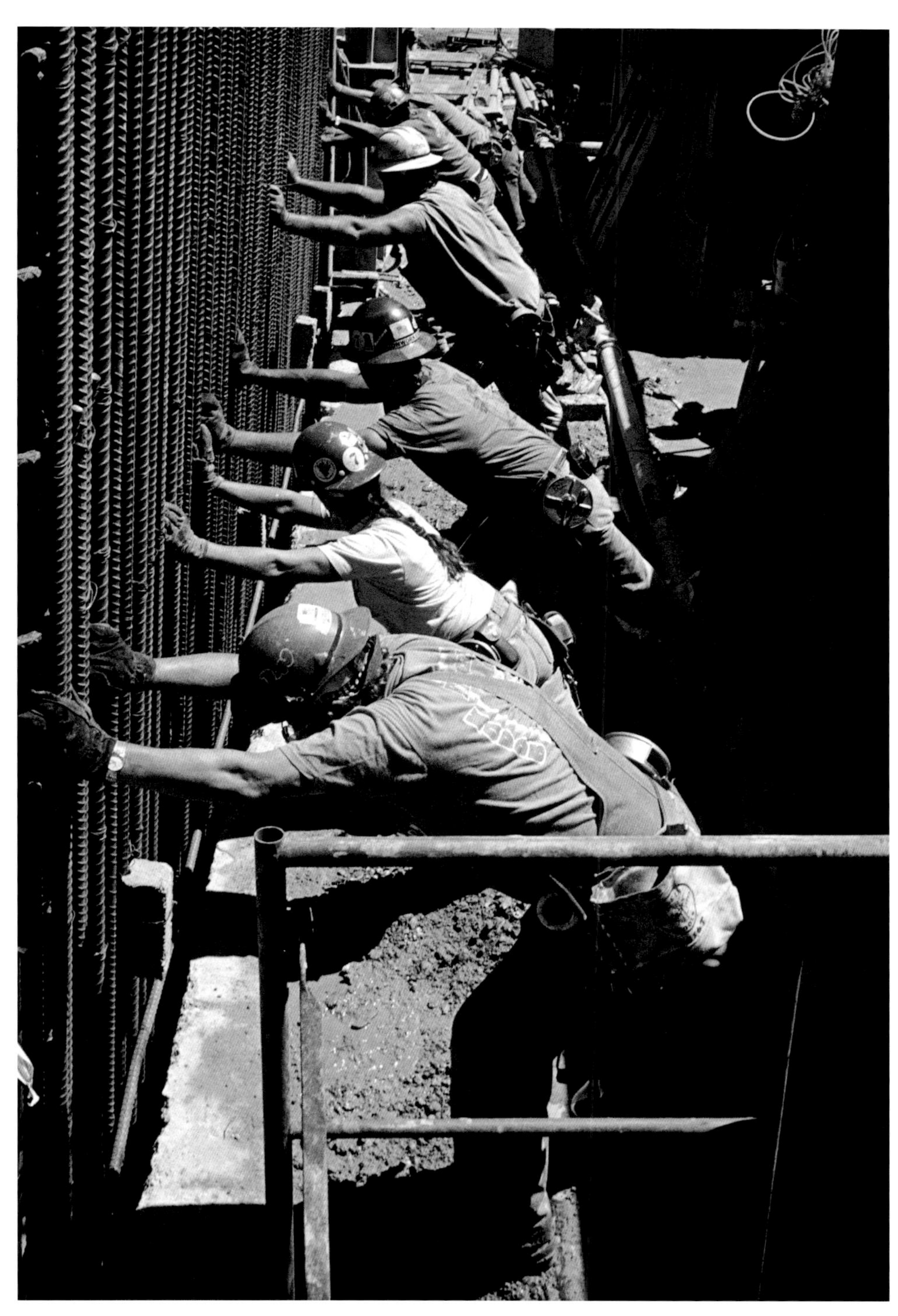

Rebar wall for ventilator
building, Atlantic Avenue
1997

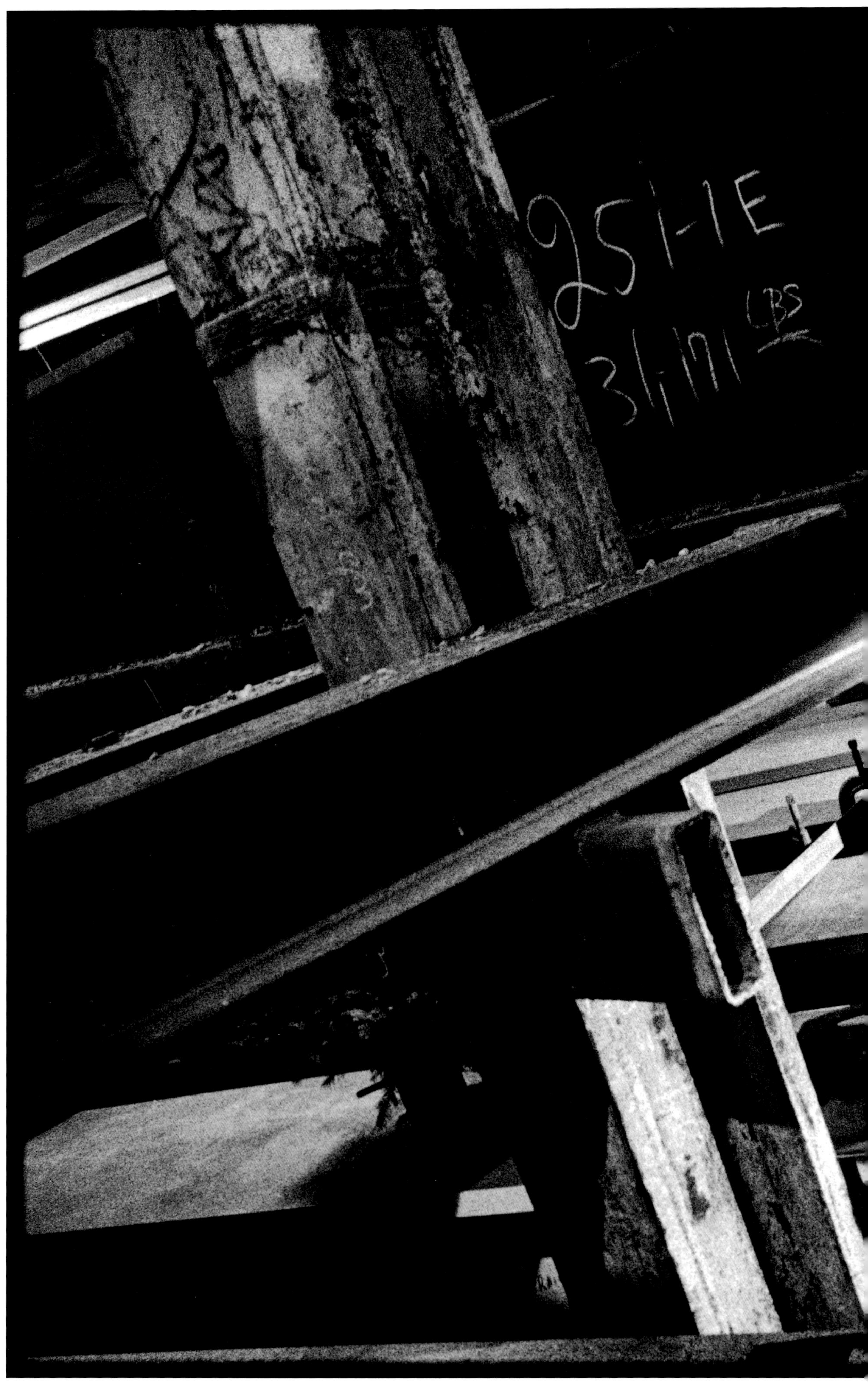

Tunnel roof beams,
Summer Street at South Station
2000

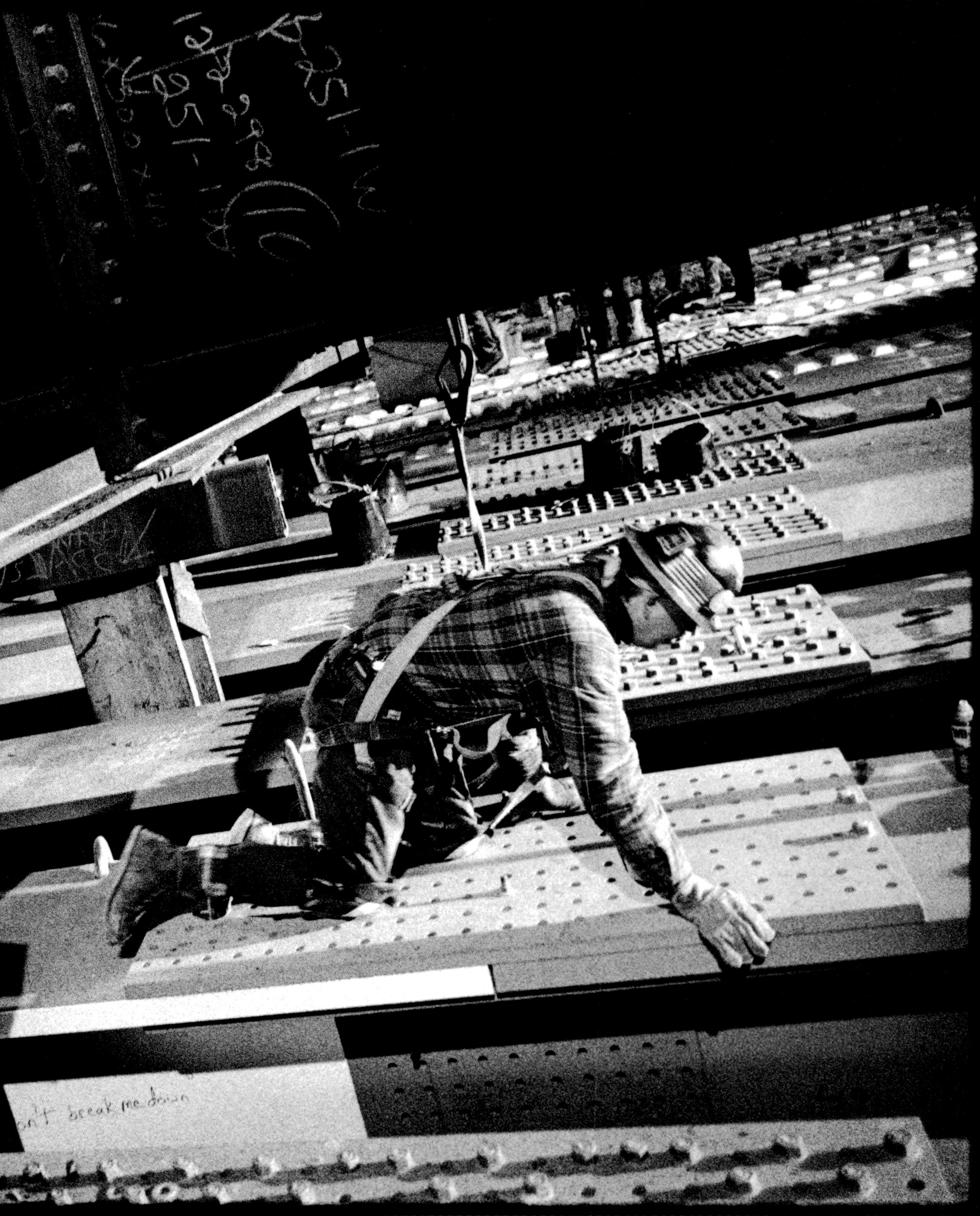

break me down

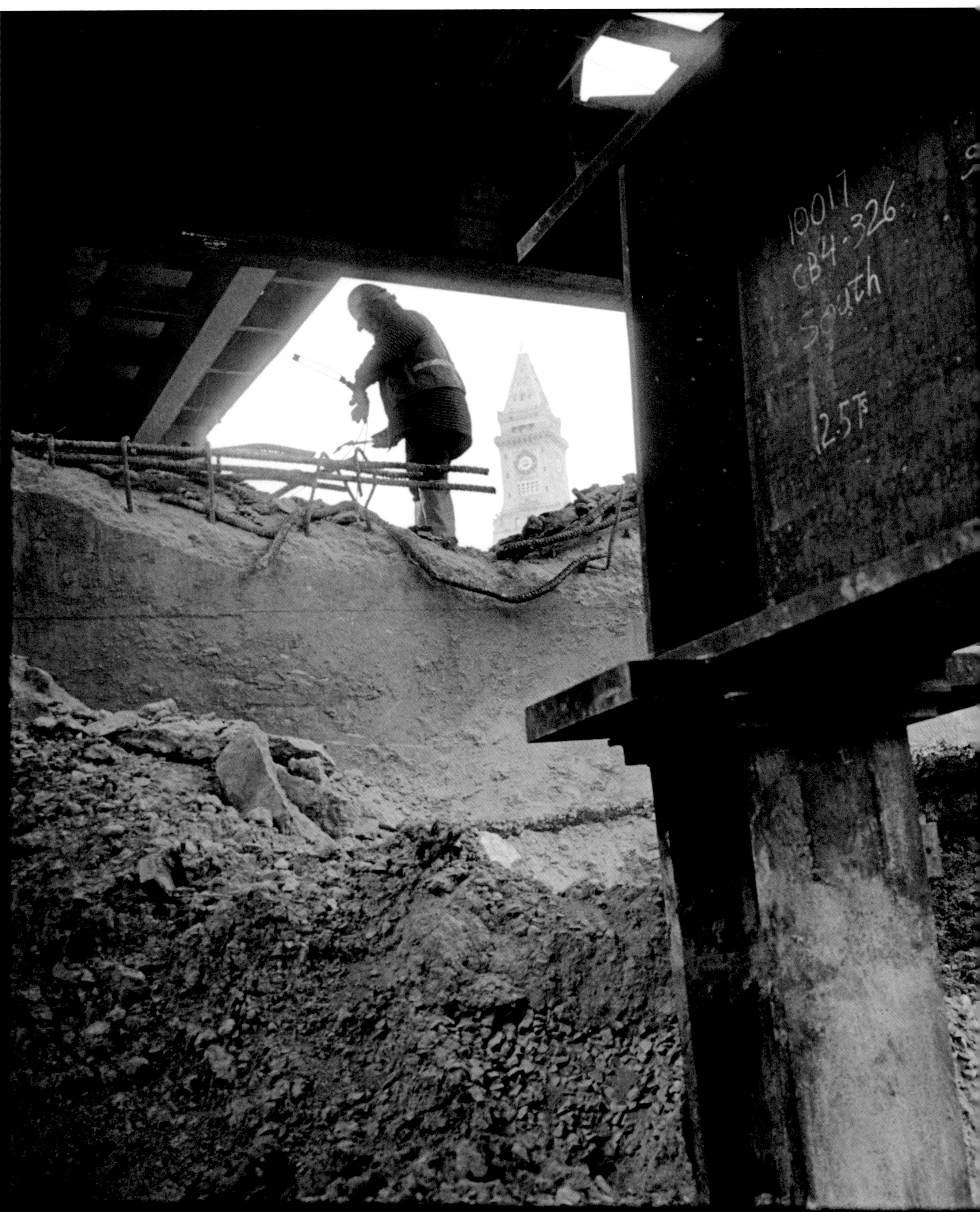
10017
CB4-326
South

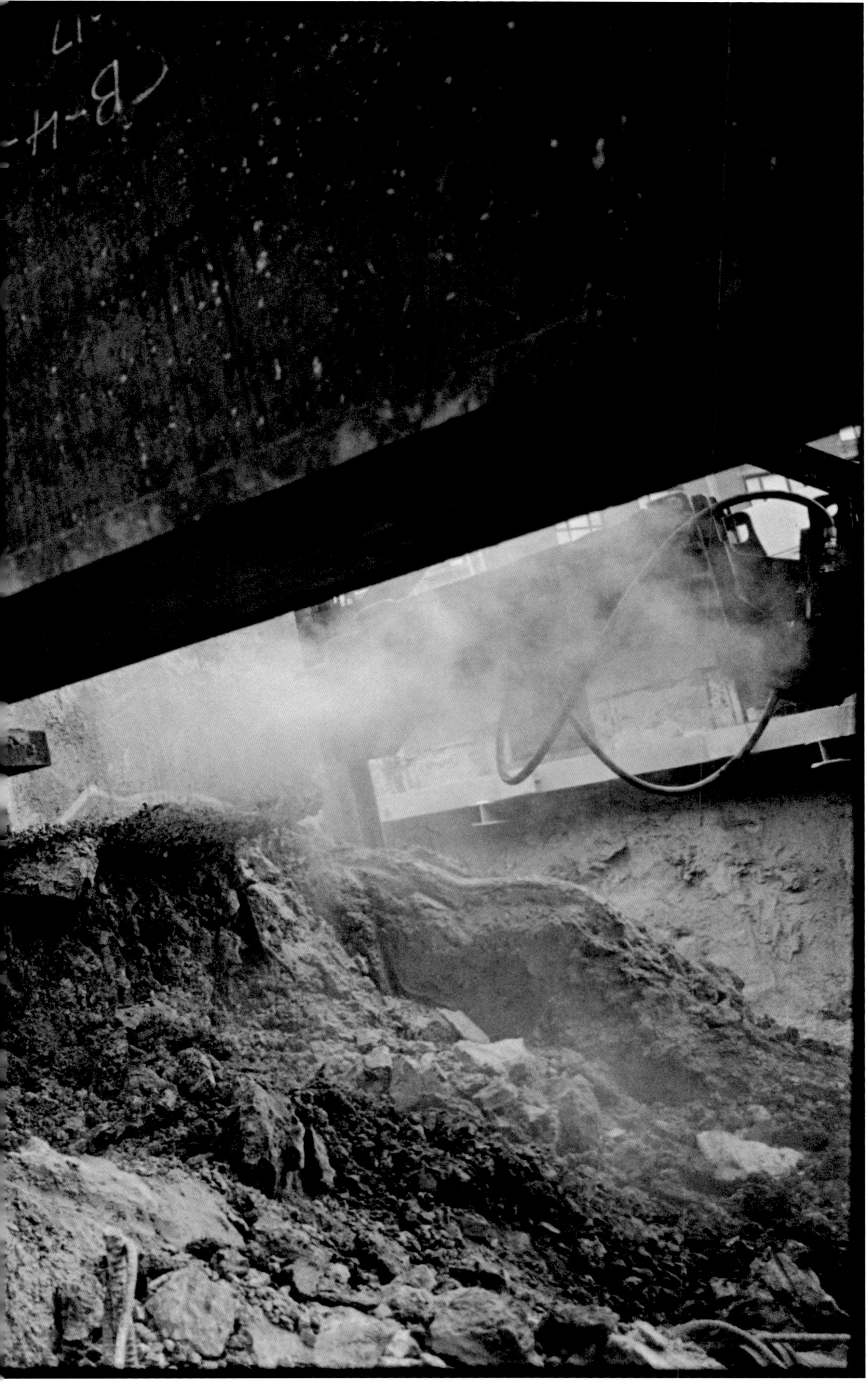

Laborer and Customs
House, near Haymarket
2000

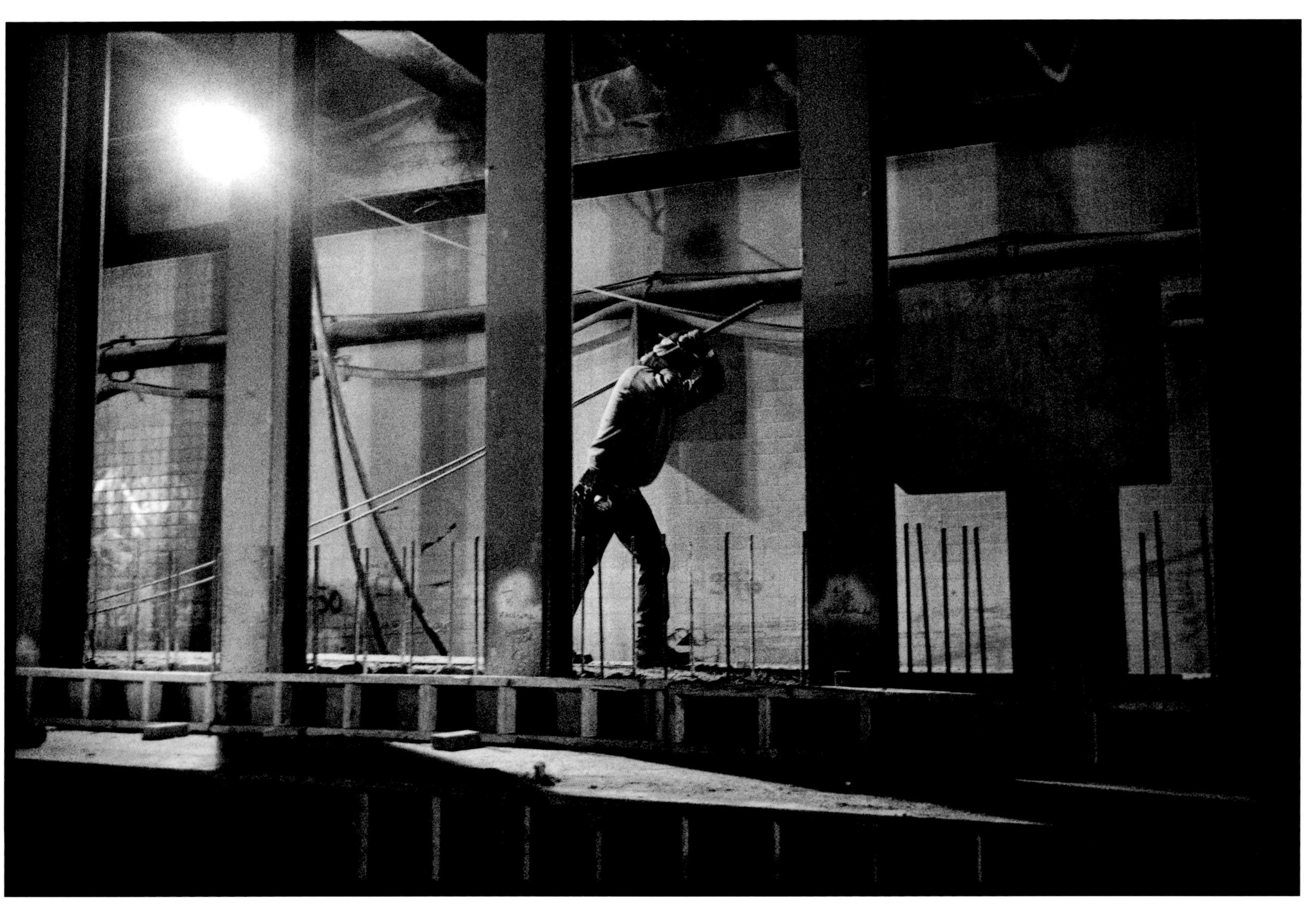

Moving rebar,
Dewey Square Tunnel
winter 2004

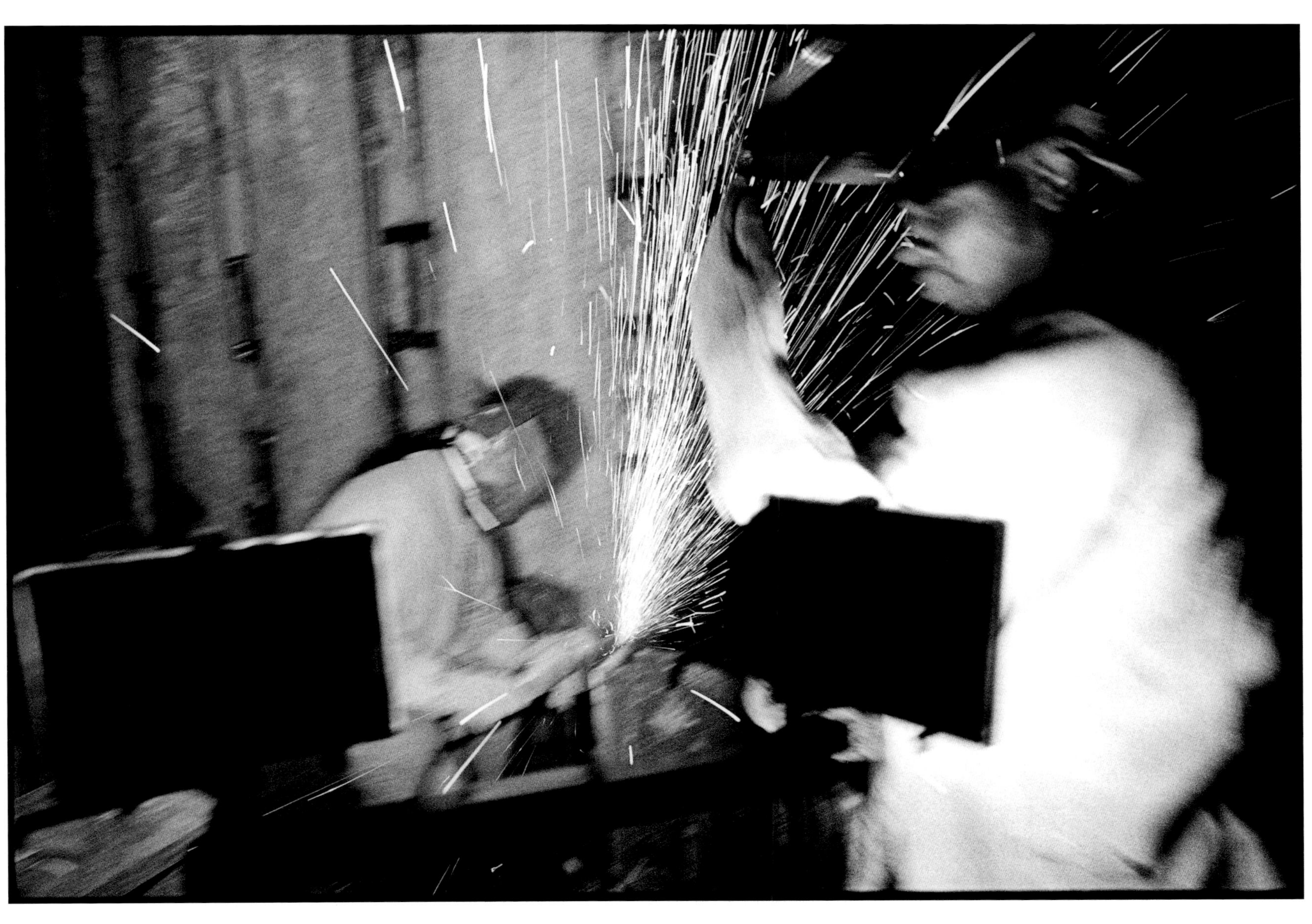

Grinding slab connector,
under Leverett Circle
2003

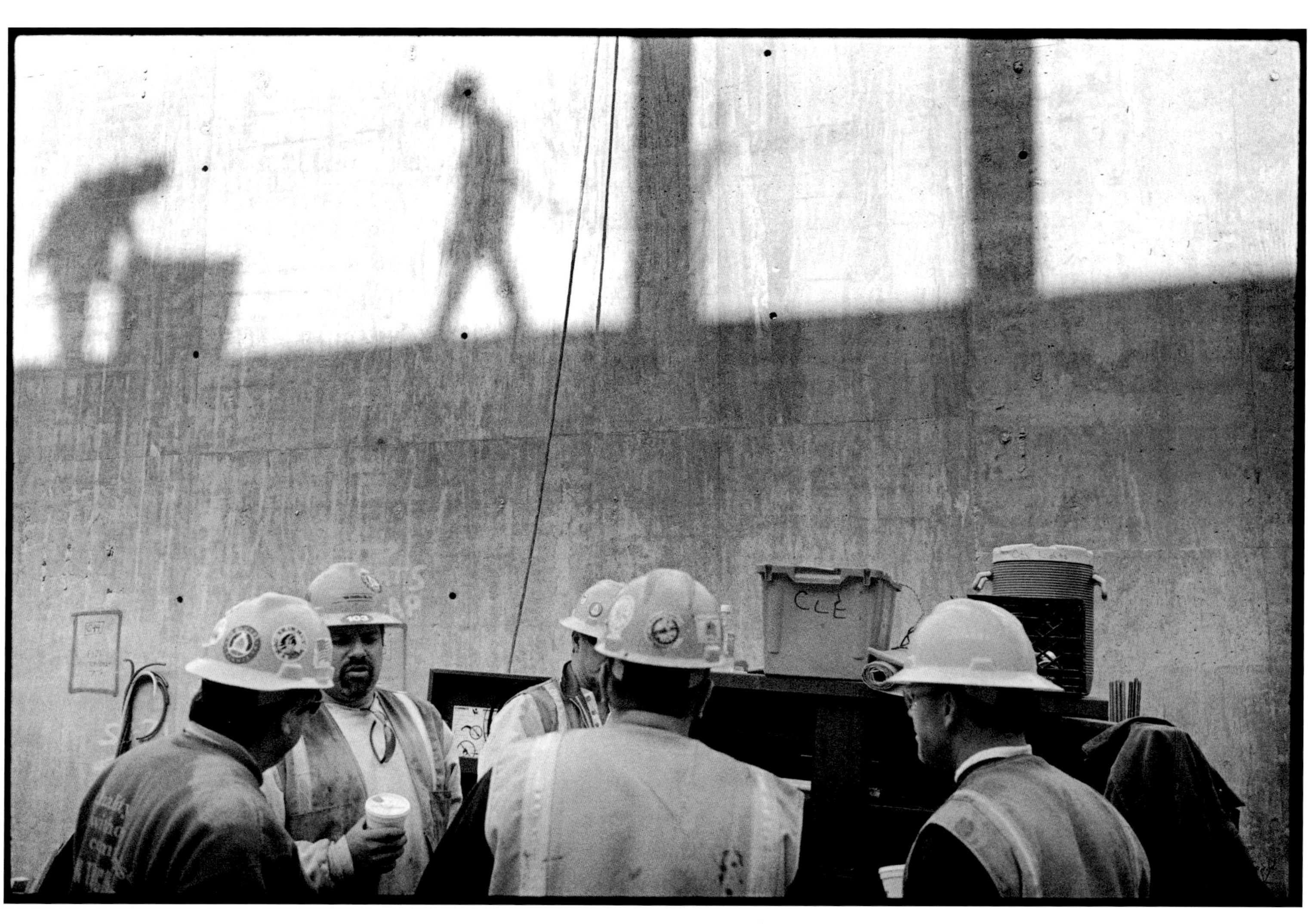

Electricians on break, near
Dewey Square Tunnel section
2003

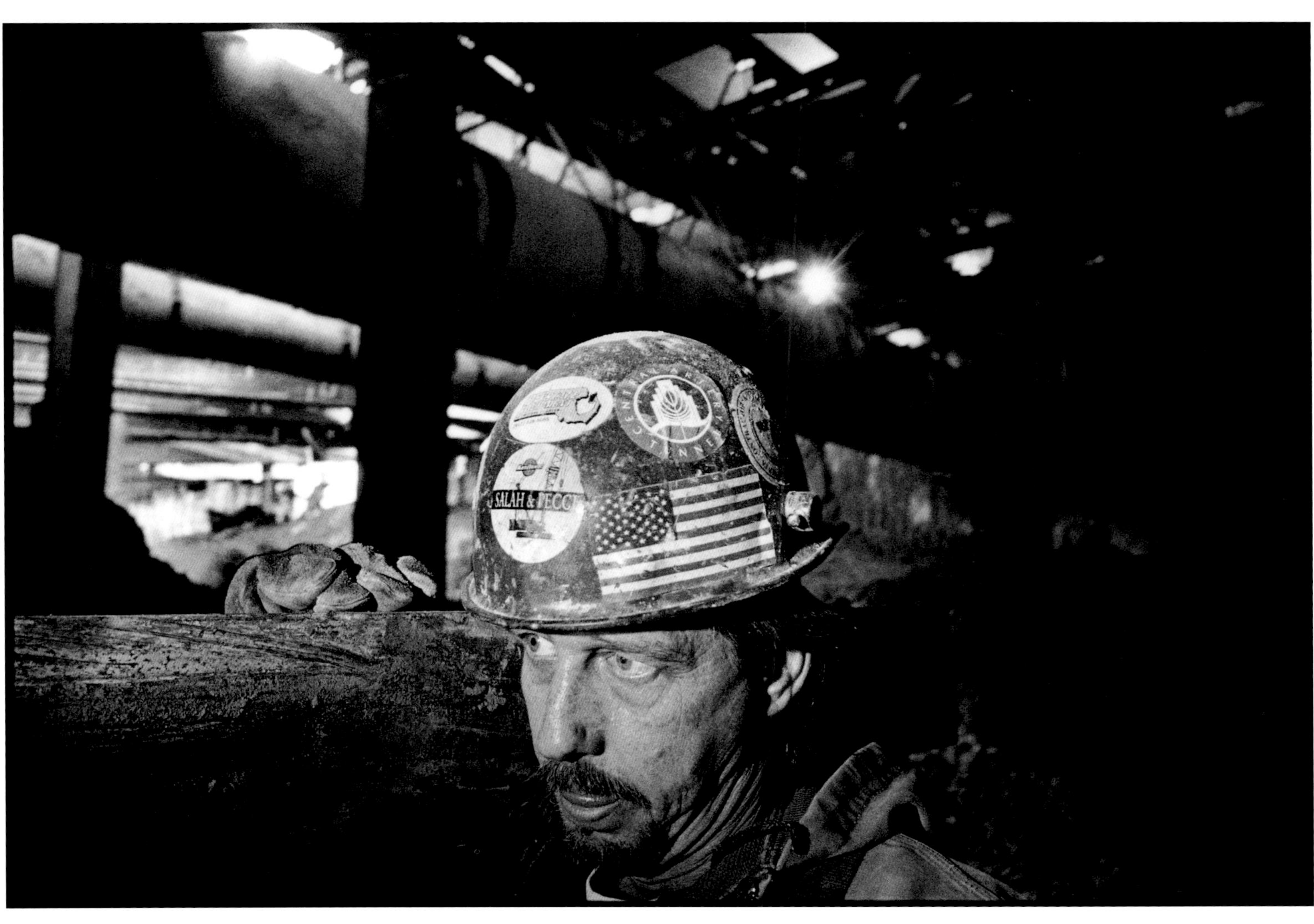

Pile driver, High Street
2003

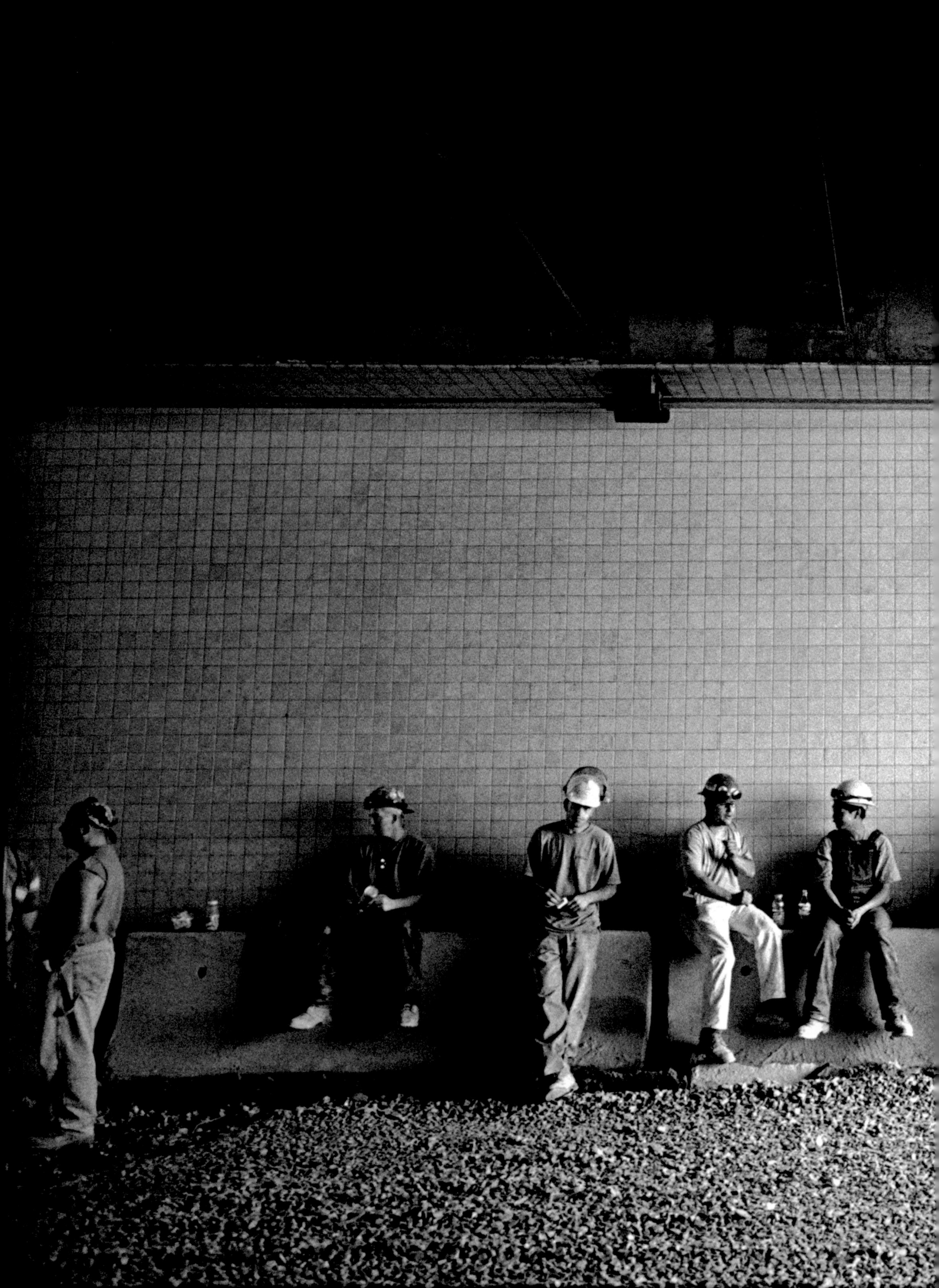

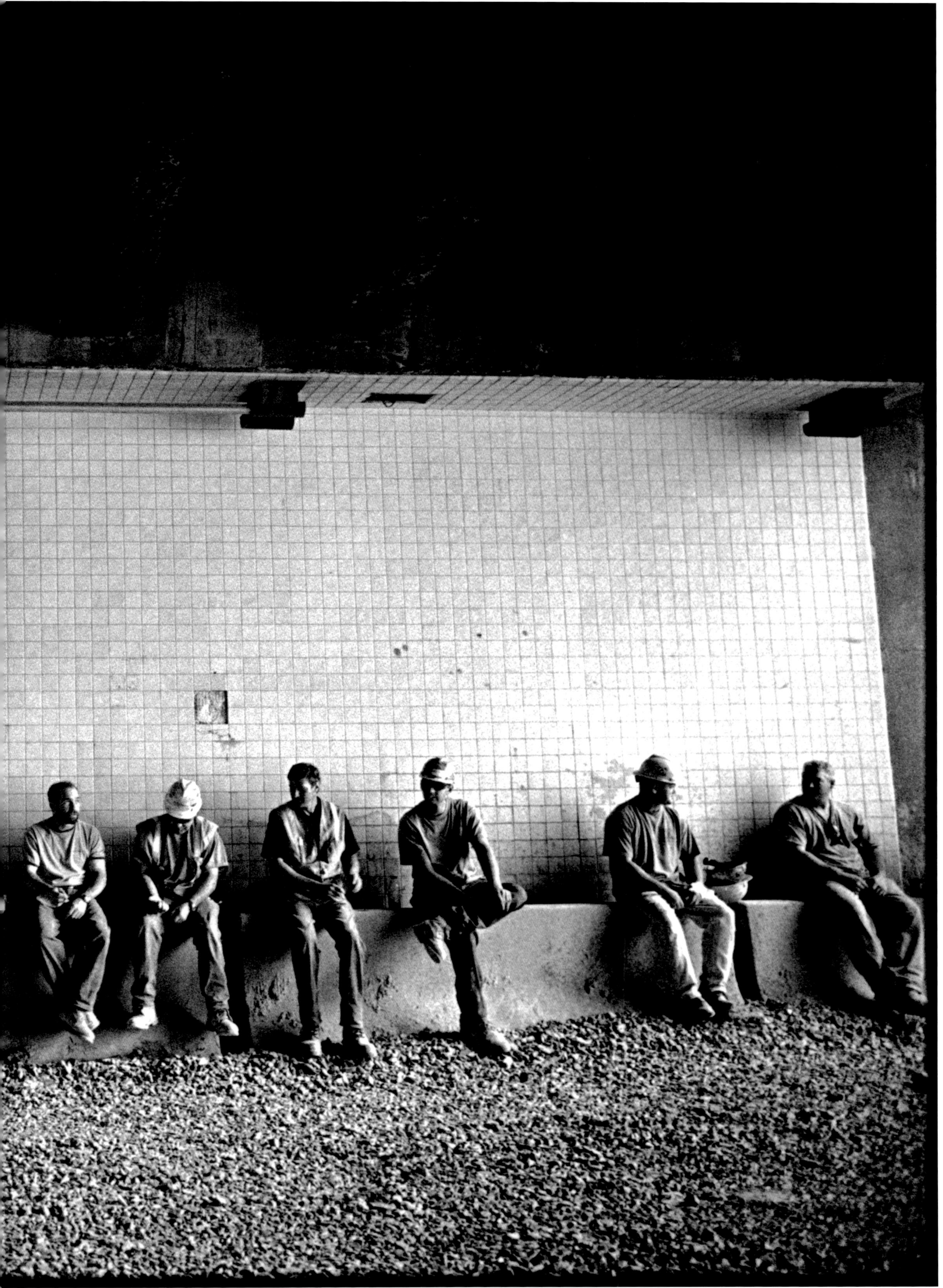

◀ Morning break, Dewey Square
2003

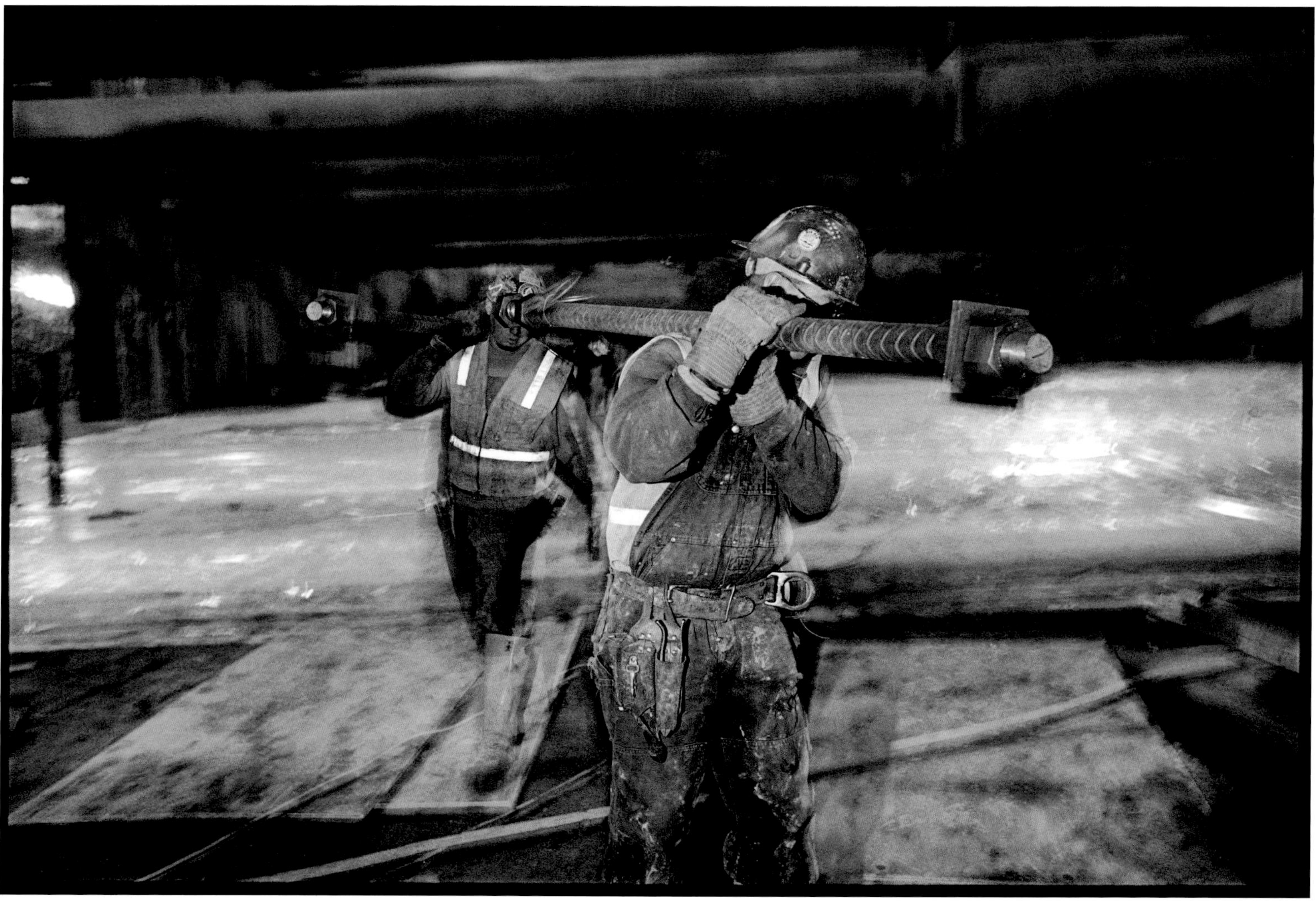

Carrying Dywidags under
Causeway Street
2001

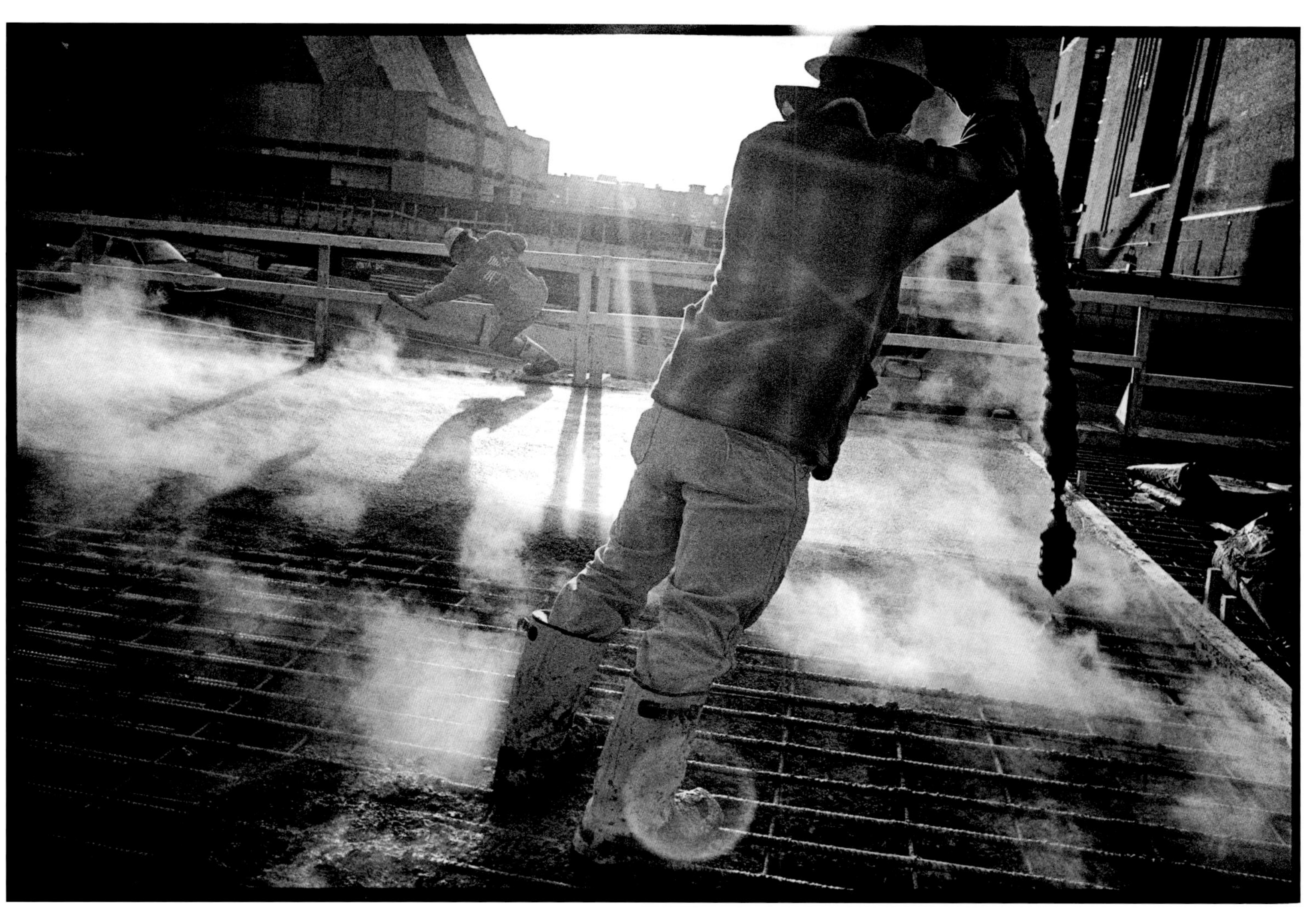

Pouring concrete next to existing
artery, near Atlantic Avenue
2003

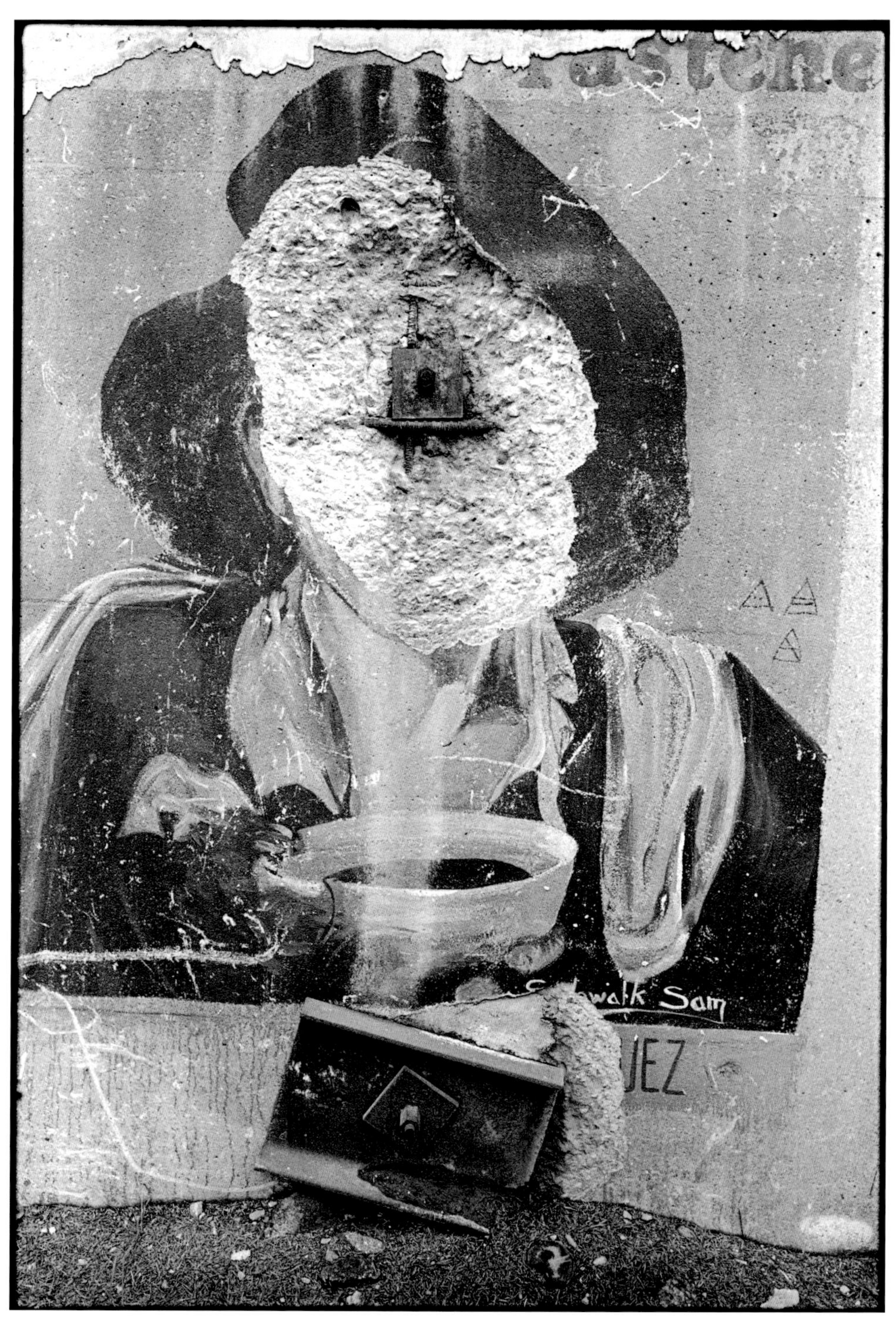

Sidewalk Sam,
Hanover Street I-93 on-ramp
2000

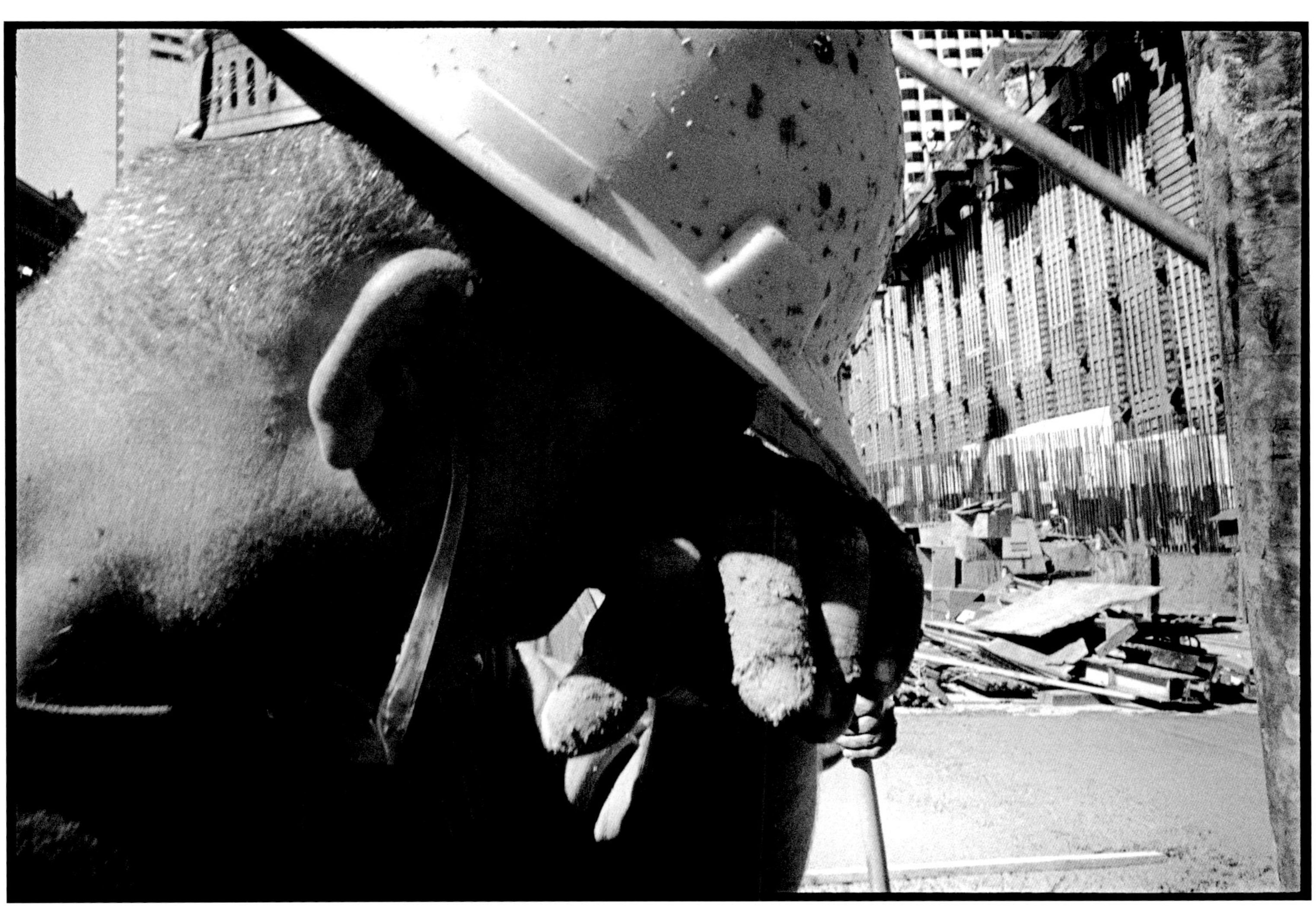

Pouring concrete,
High Street
2003

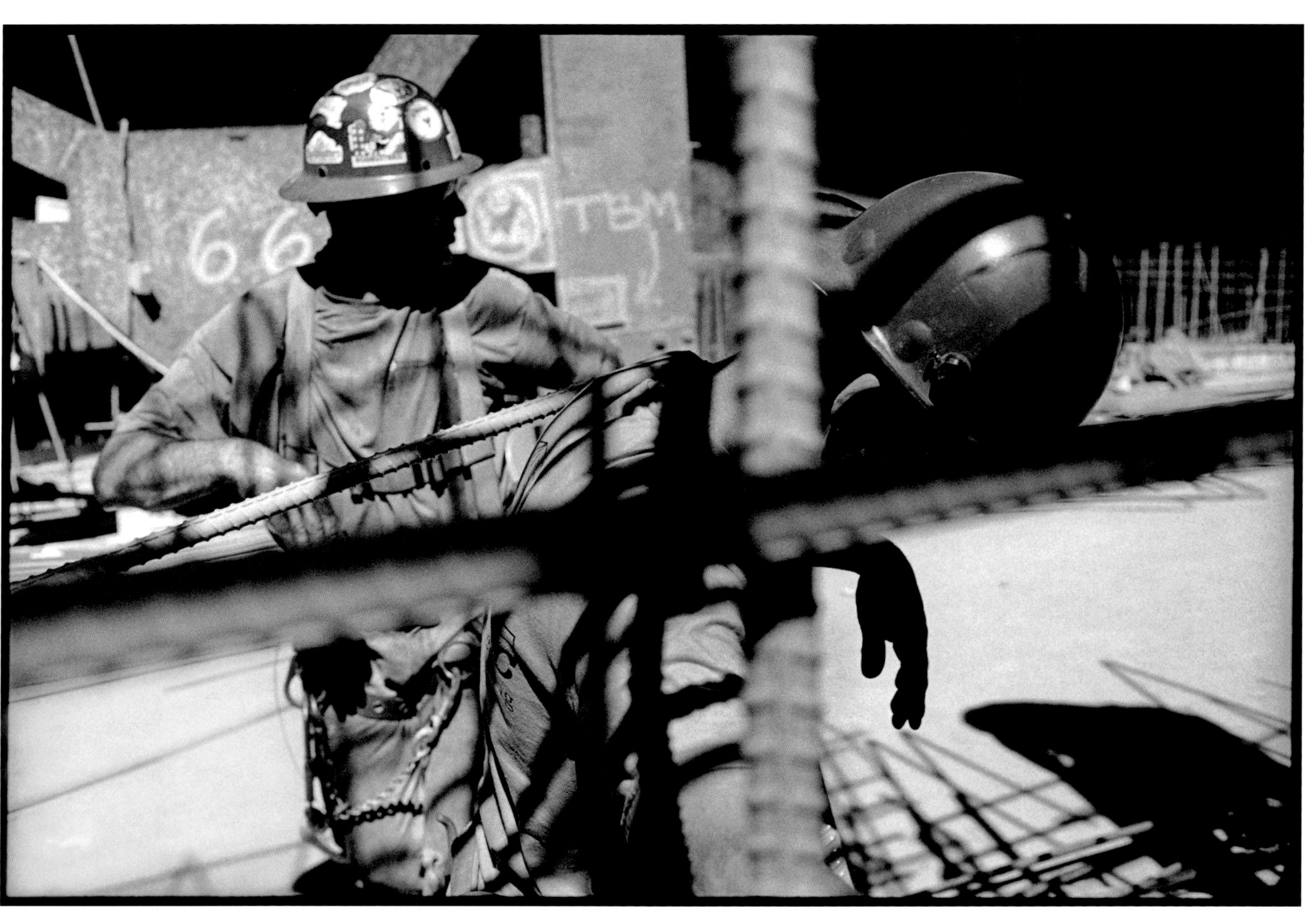

Atlantic Avenue
summer 2001

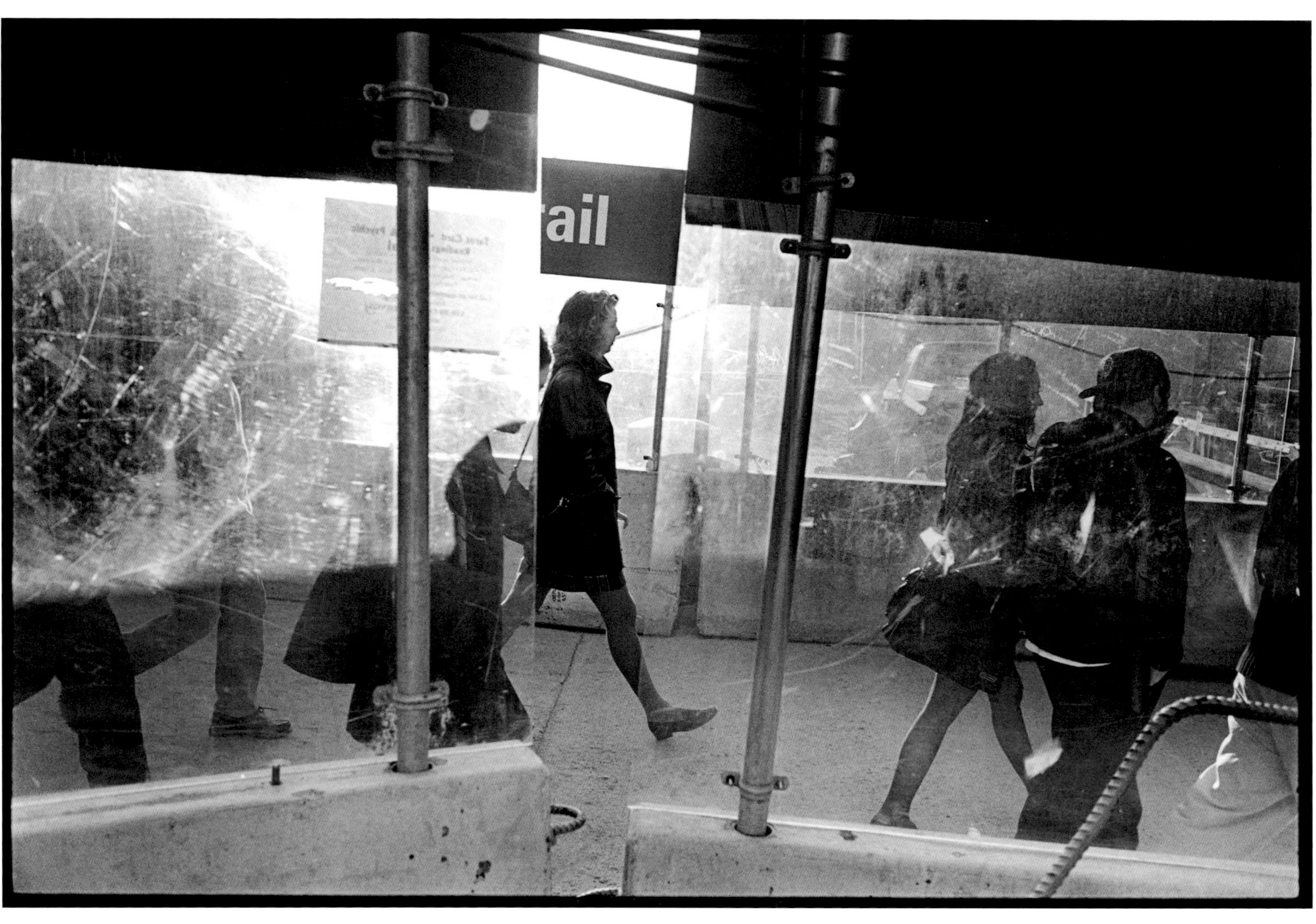

Commuters,
the Freedom Trail
2000

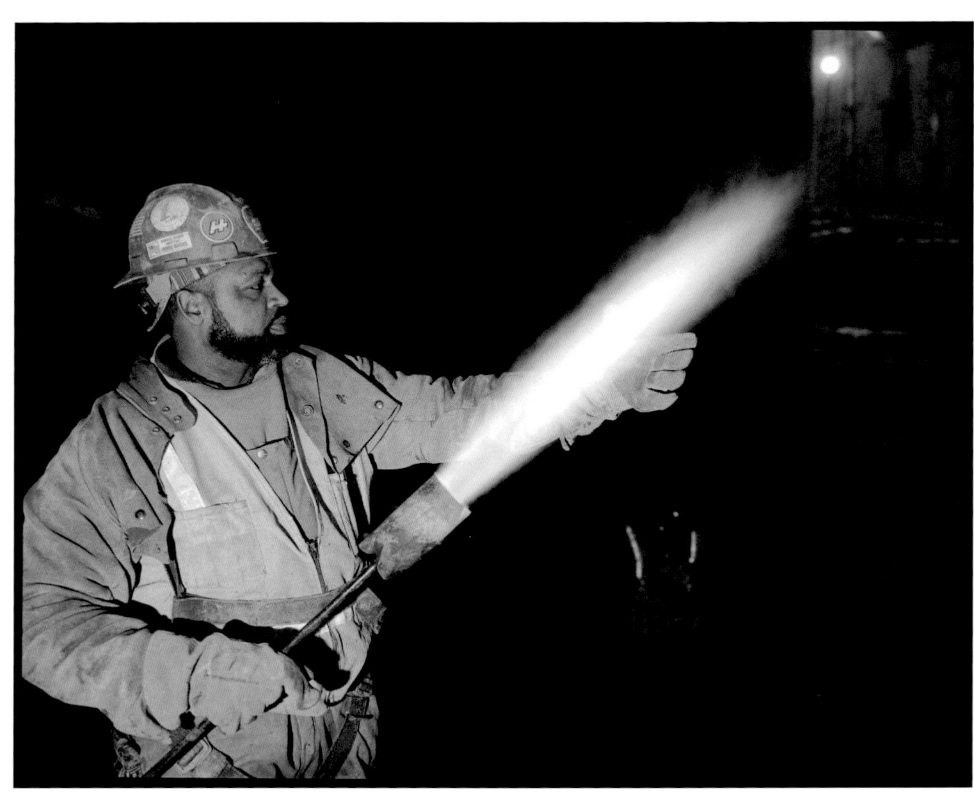

Thawing frozen glove, under
North Washington Street
2001

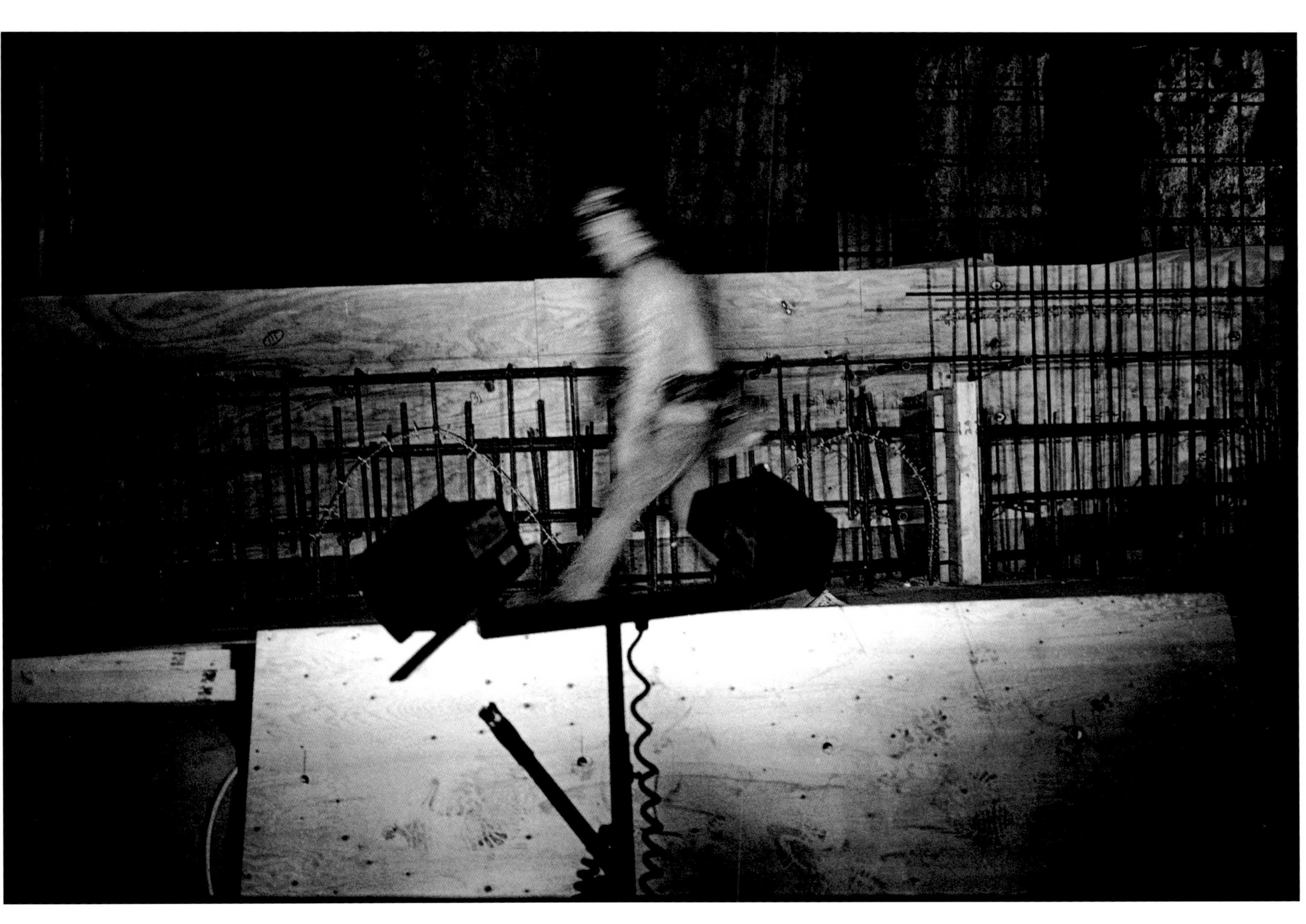

Work lights, under
Causeway Street
2002

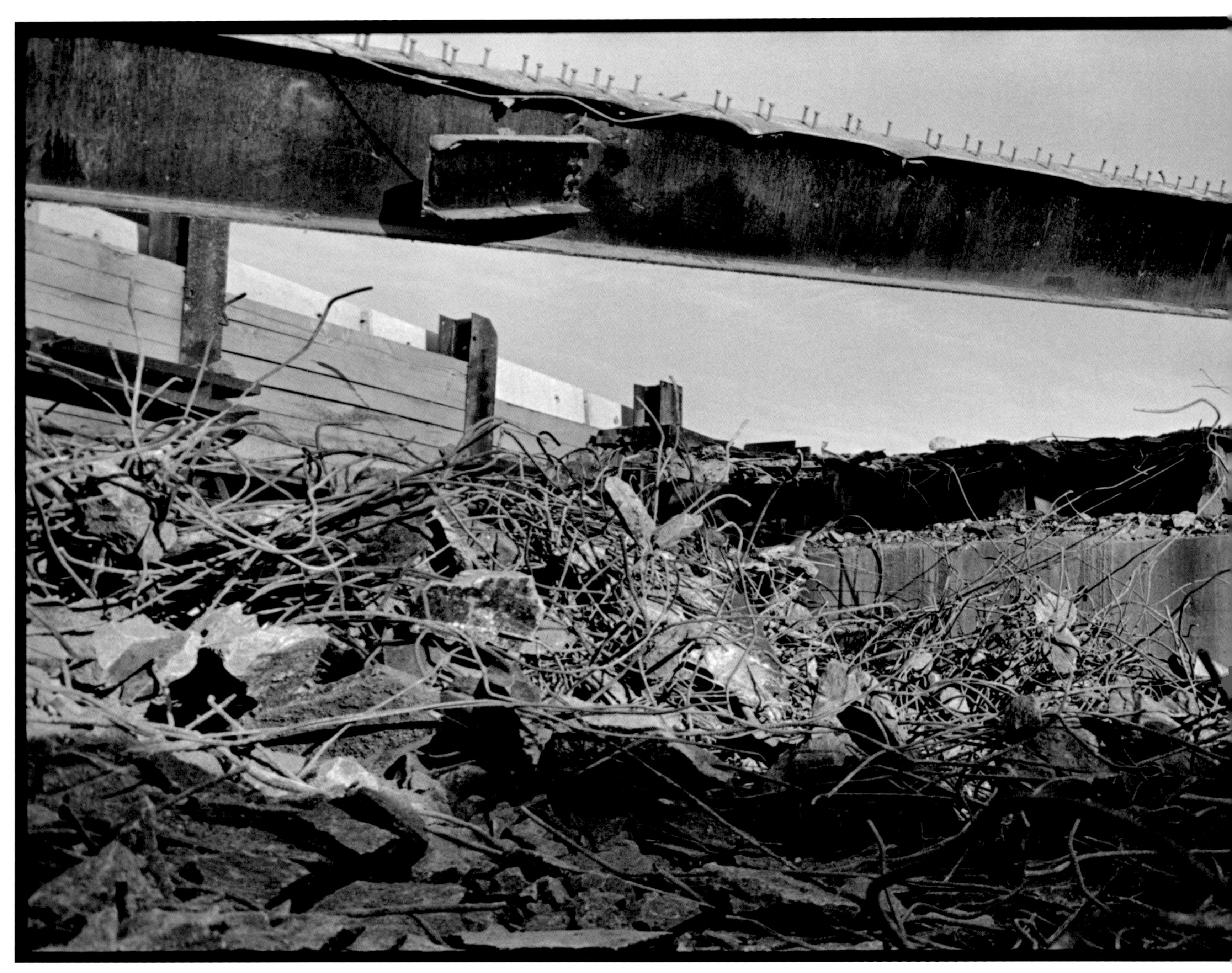

Demolition of the southbound
artery, south of Chinatown
1999

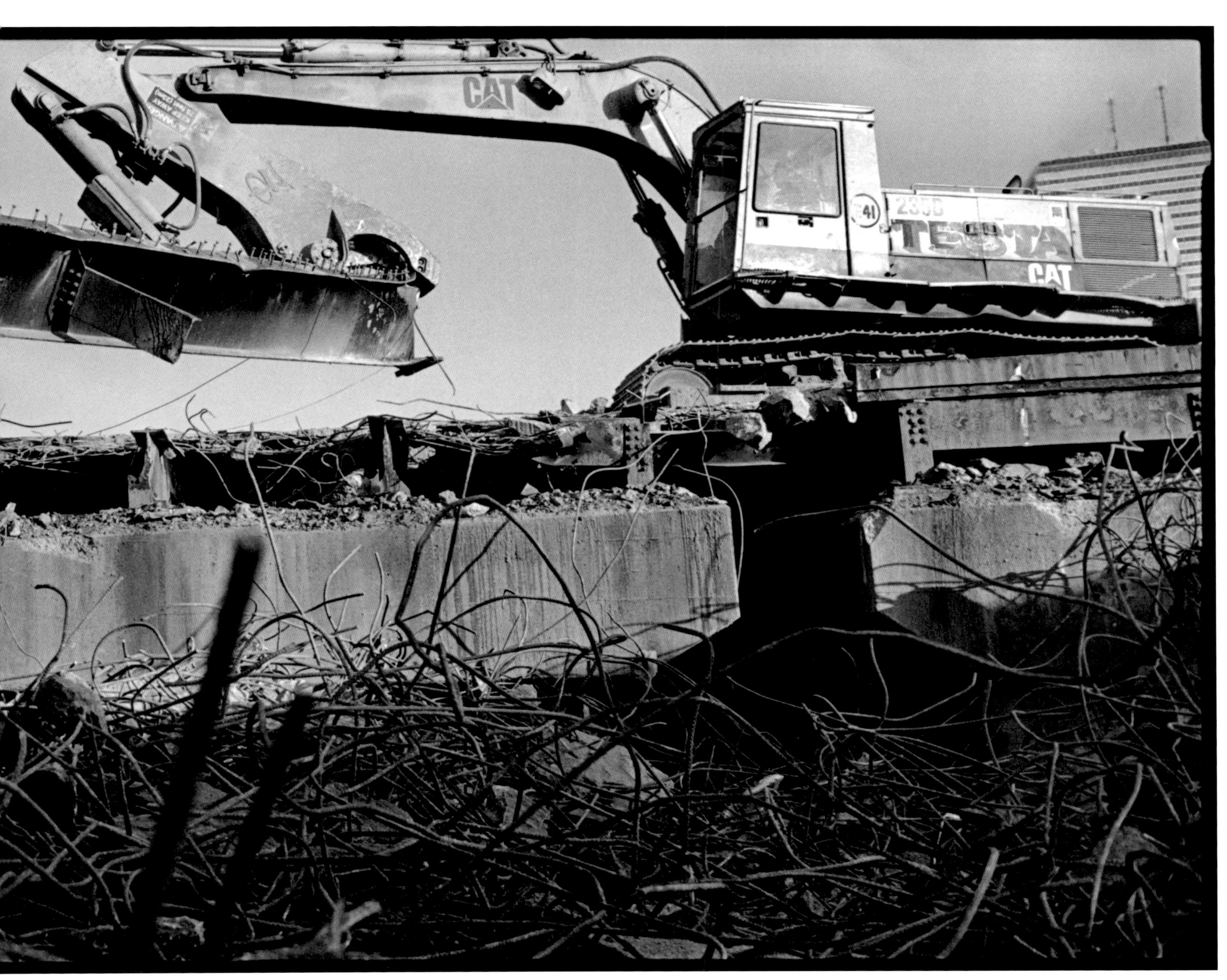
CAT
41
TESTA
CAT

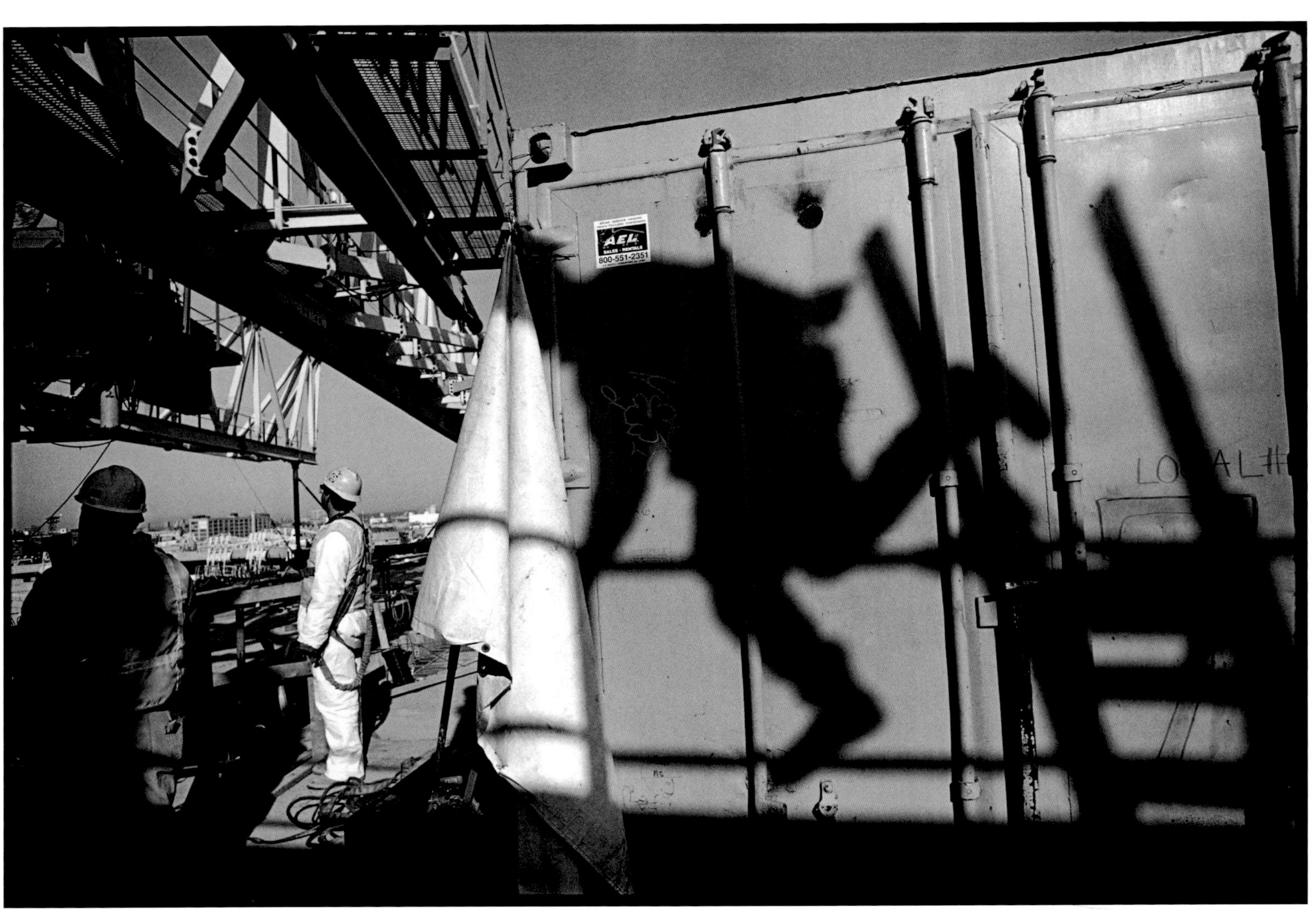

Shadow, Charlestown
2001

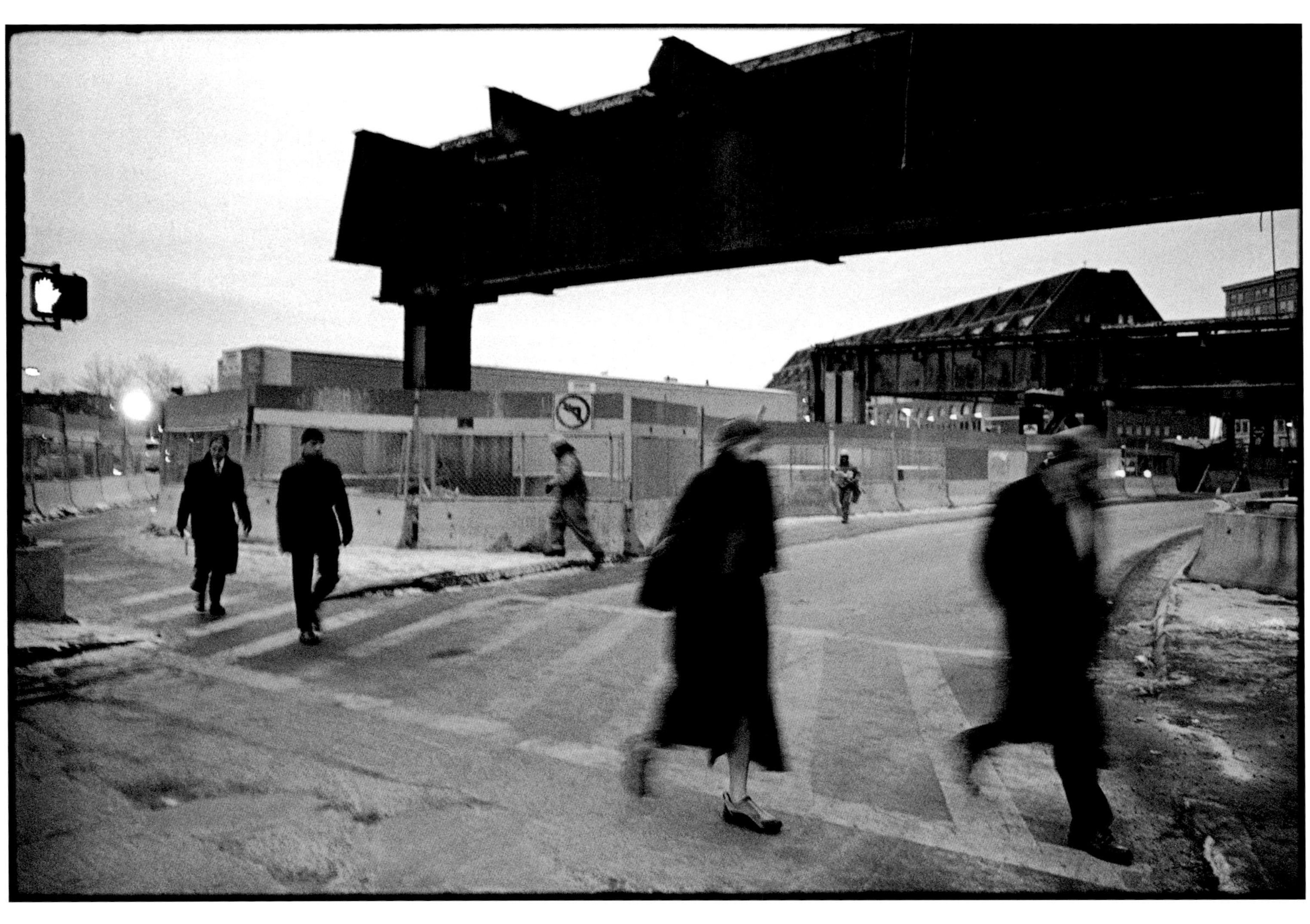

Commuters crossing the
surface artery with demolition
underway
2004

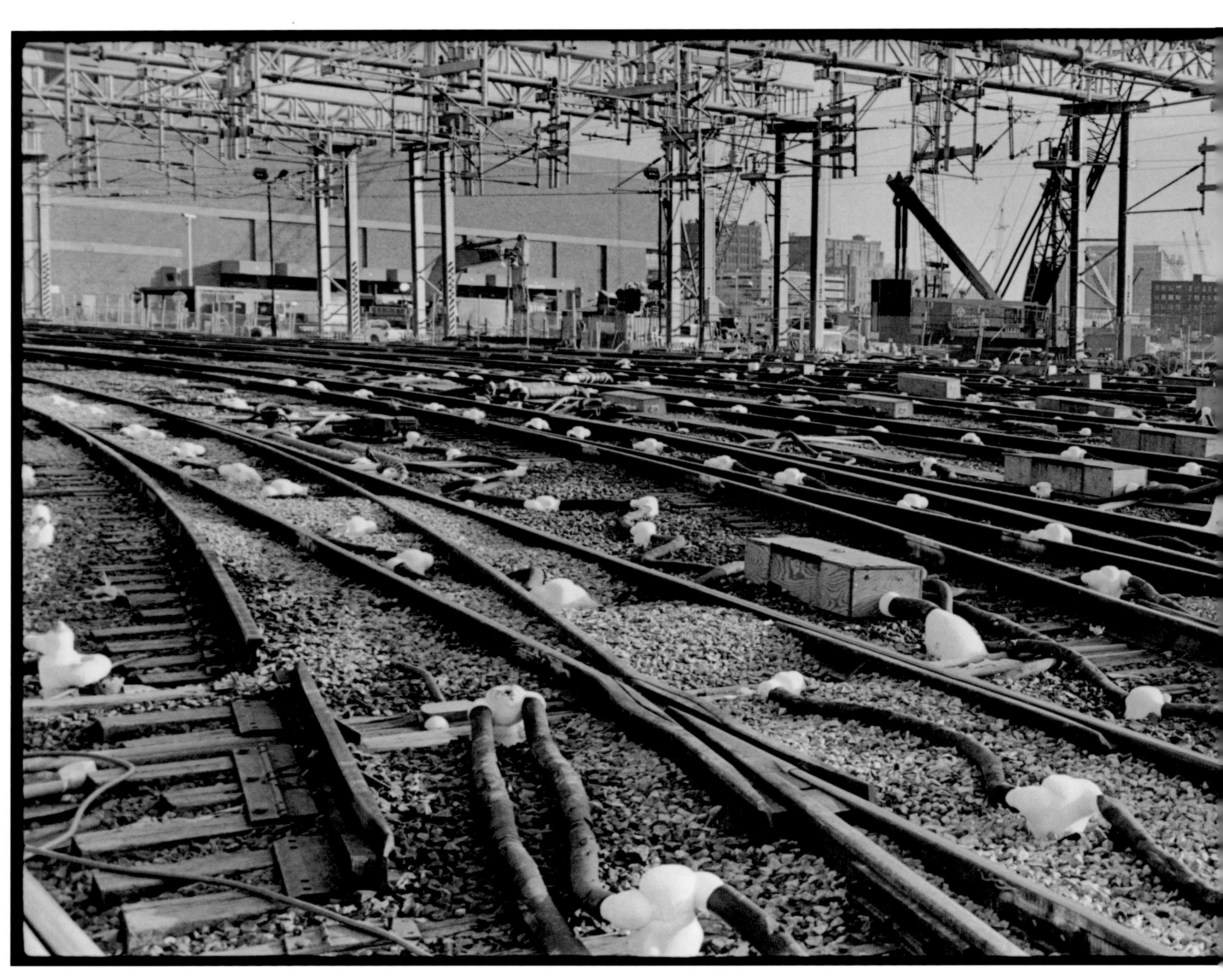

Tracks at South Station with
ground-freezing fixtures in place
1999

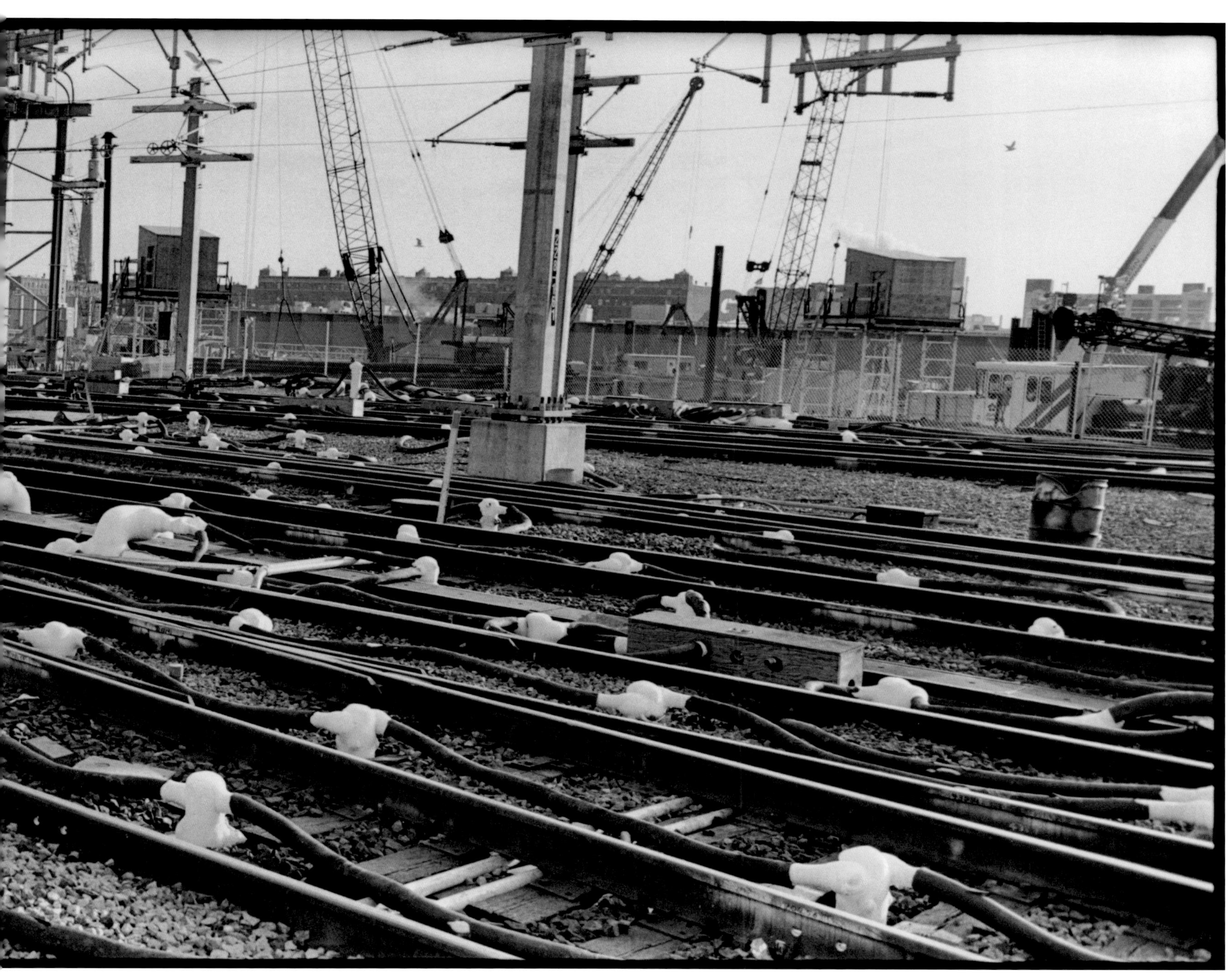

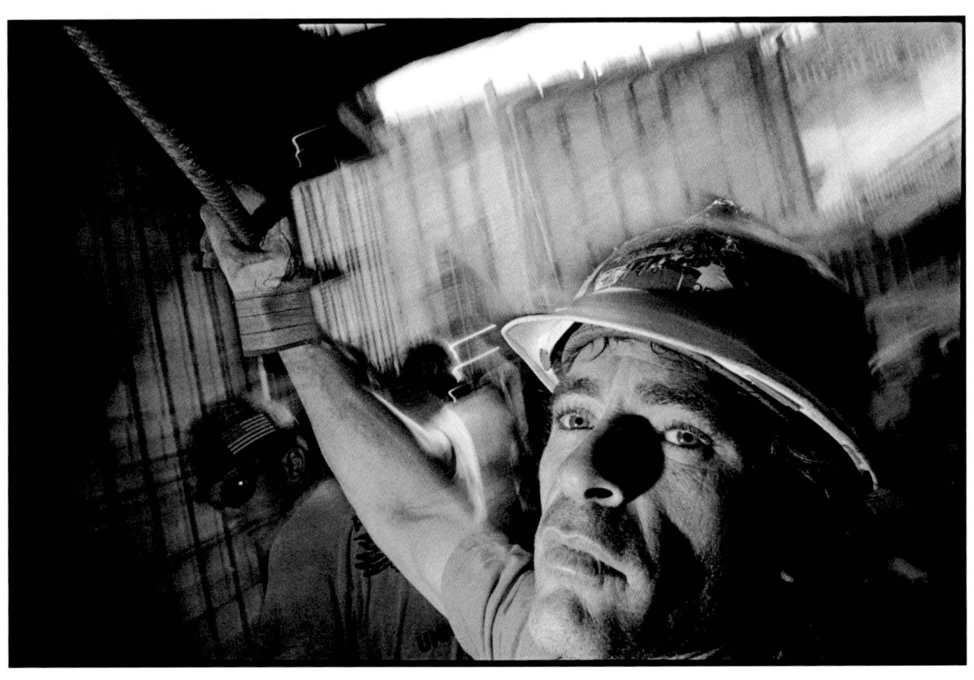

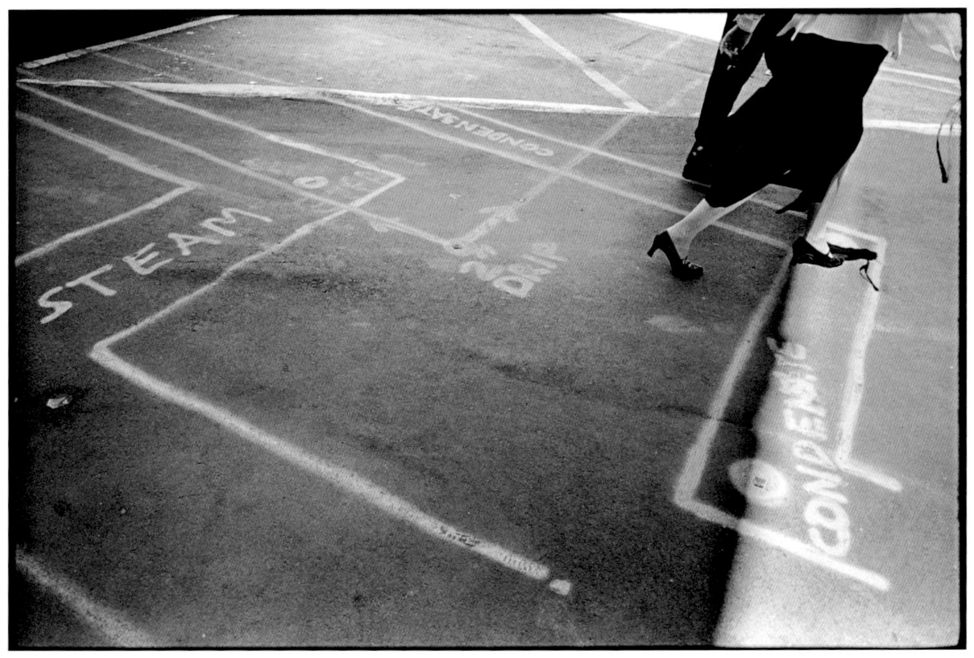

Iron worker, near High Street, 2003

"Dig Safe" markings on Broad Street, 2001

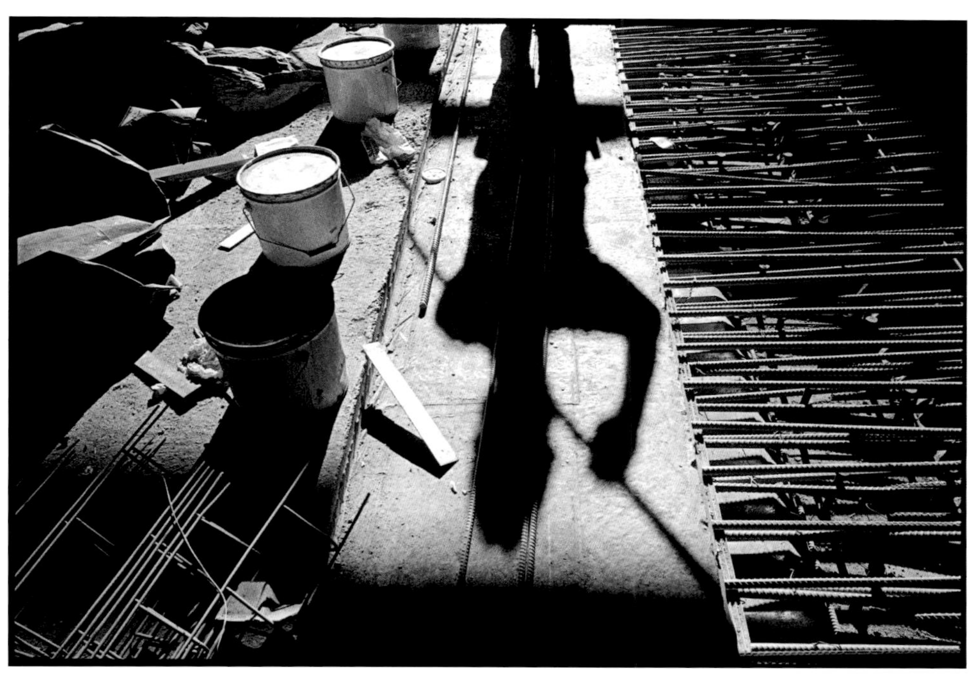

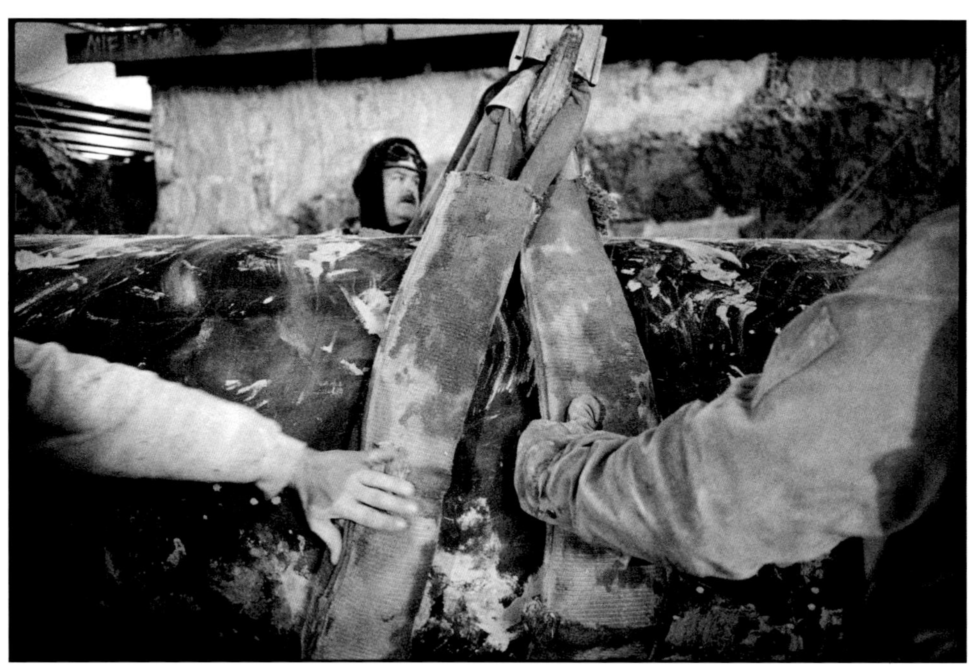

Shadow, near Atlantic Avenue, 2003

Pile drivers, winter, North Washington Street, 2000

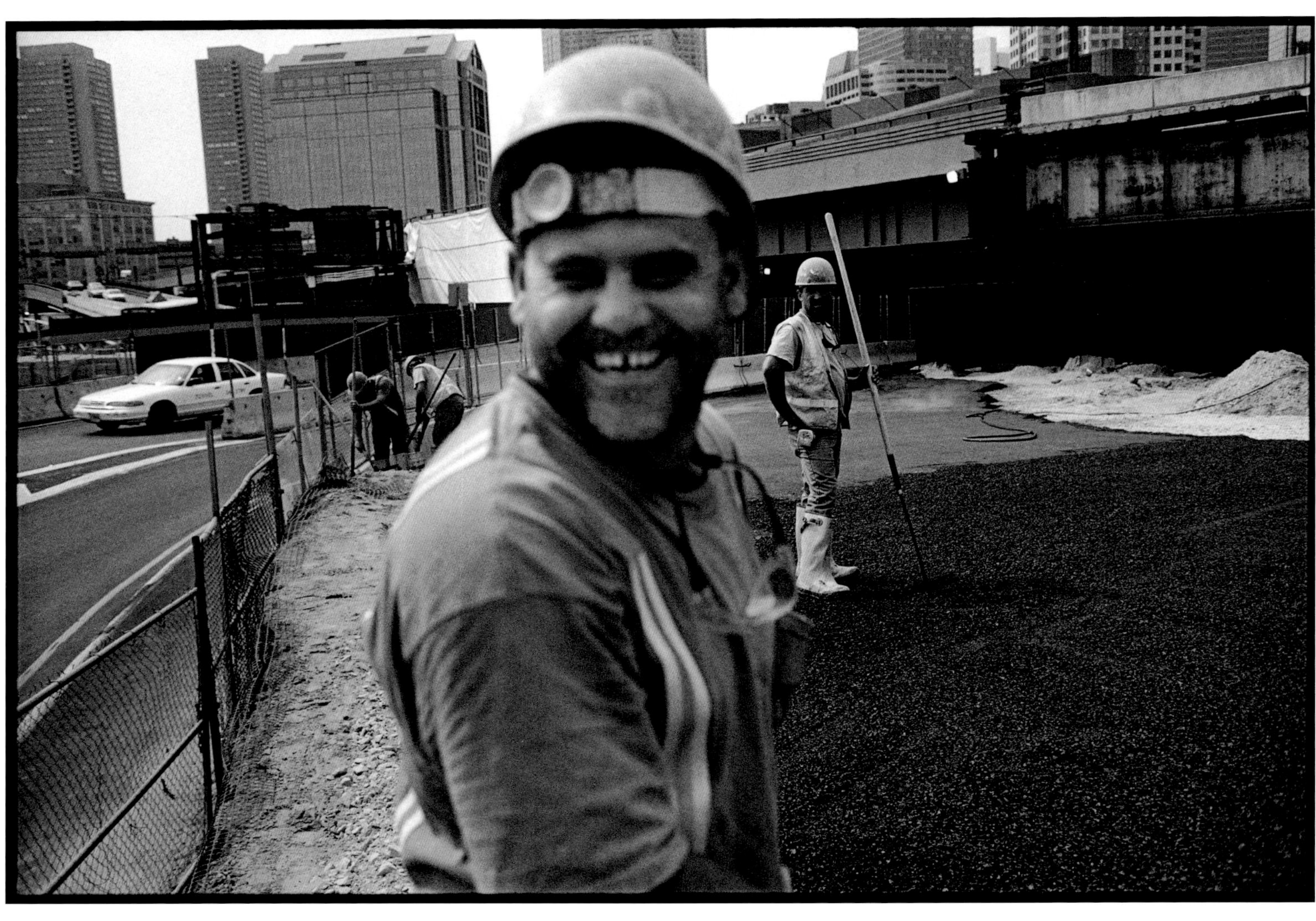

Laborer, Dock Square
2002

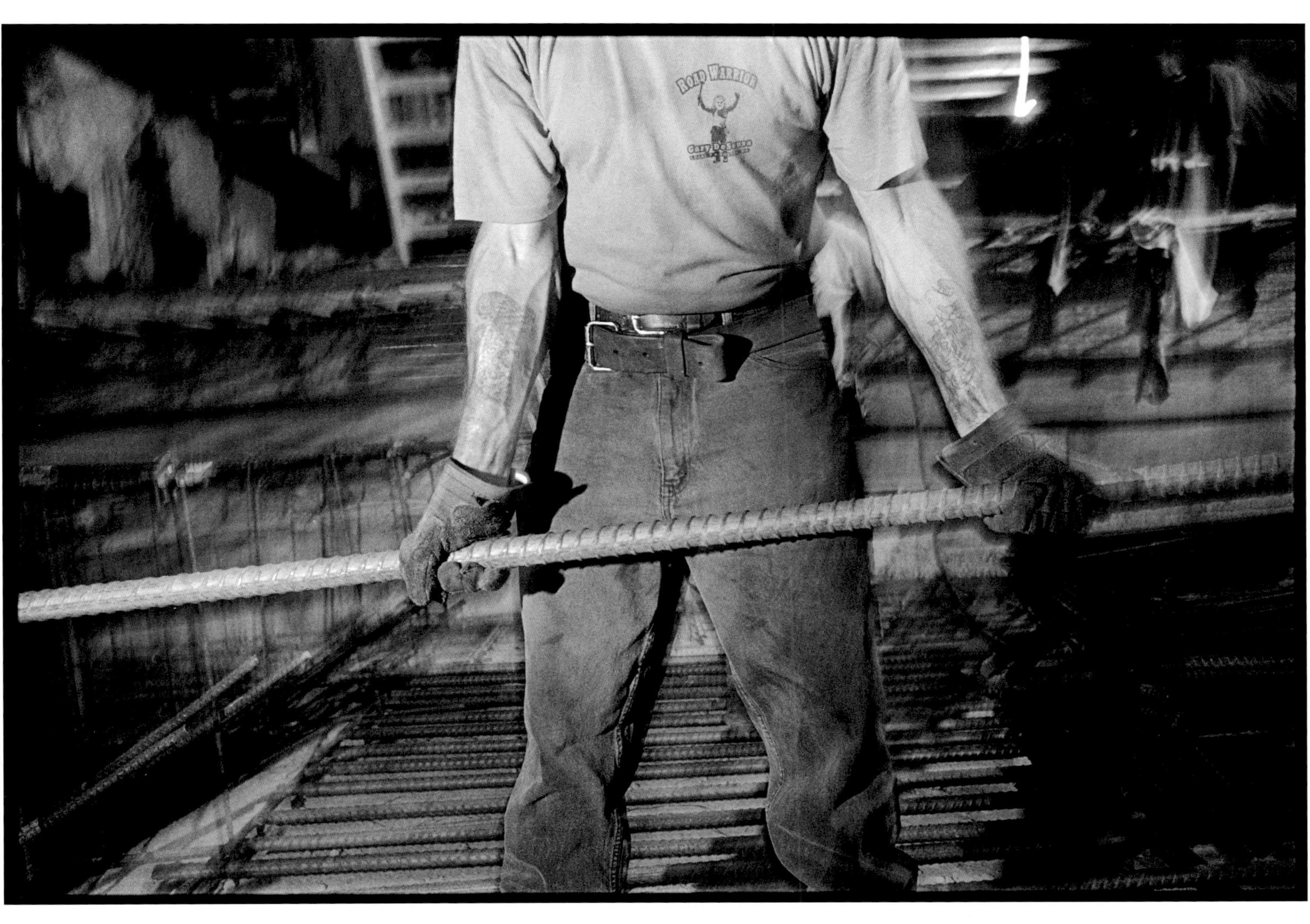

Arms and rebar,
near Haymarket
2000

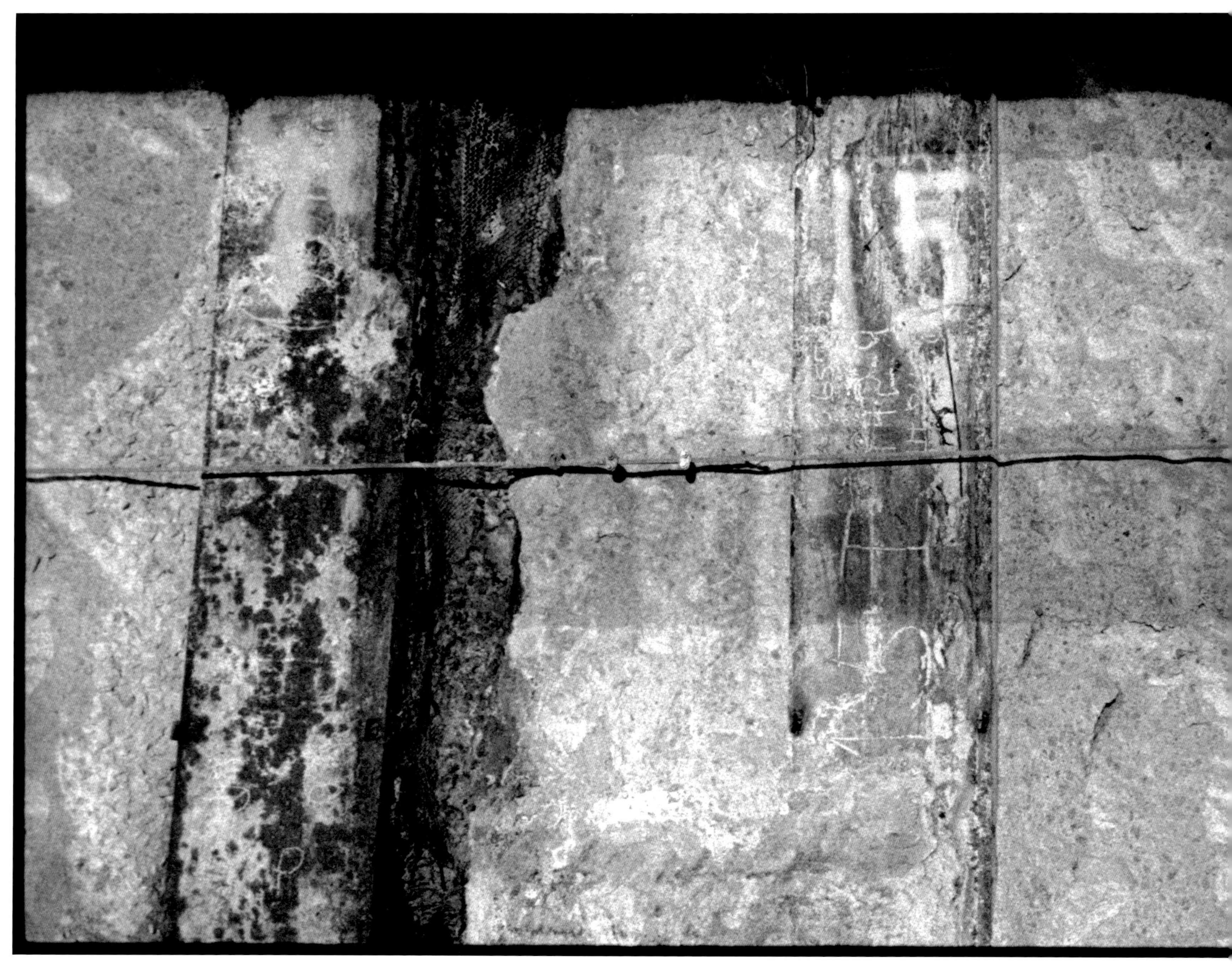

Slurry wall, near Broad Street
1999

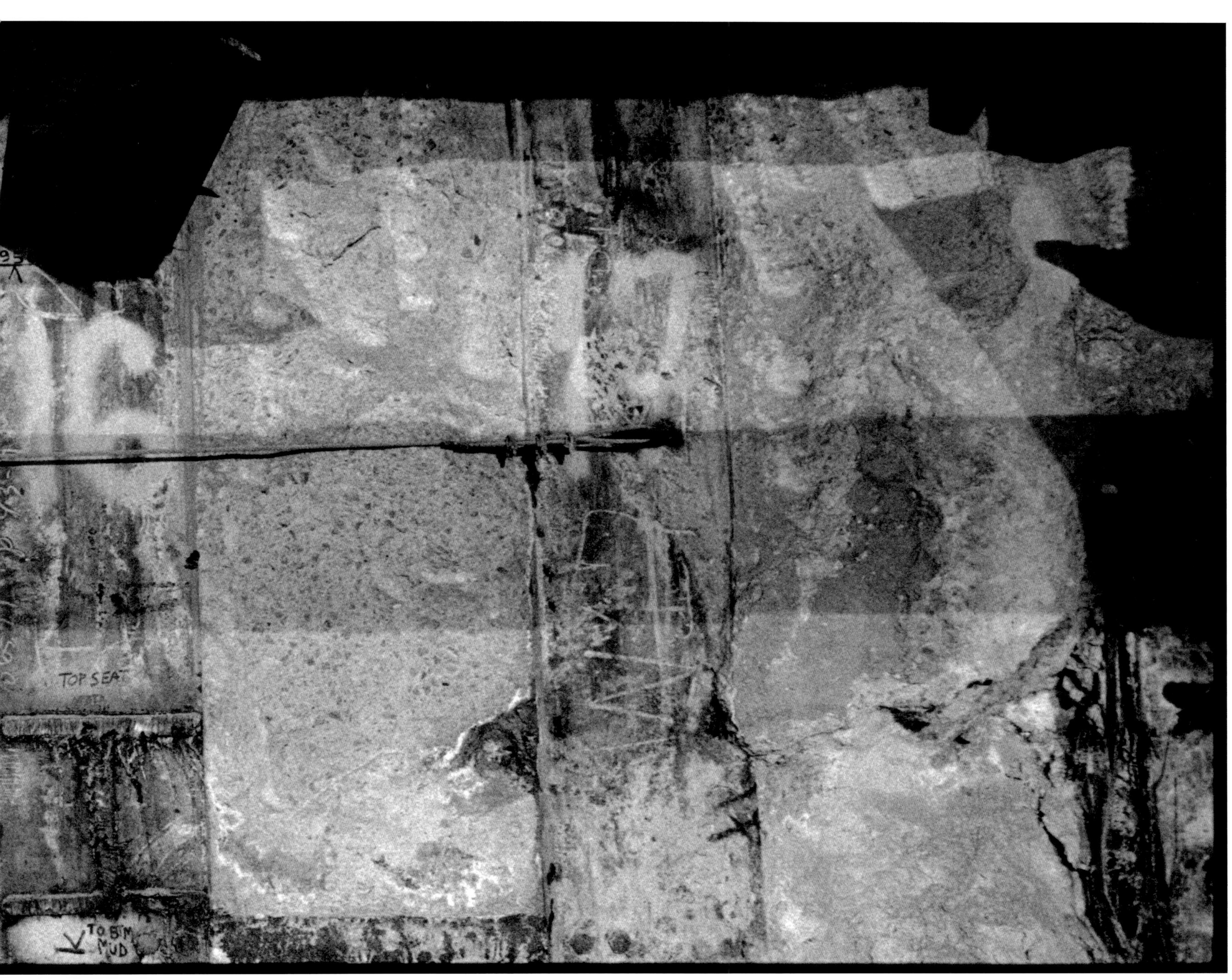
TOP SEAT
TO BTM
MUD

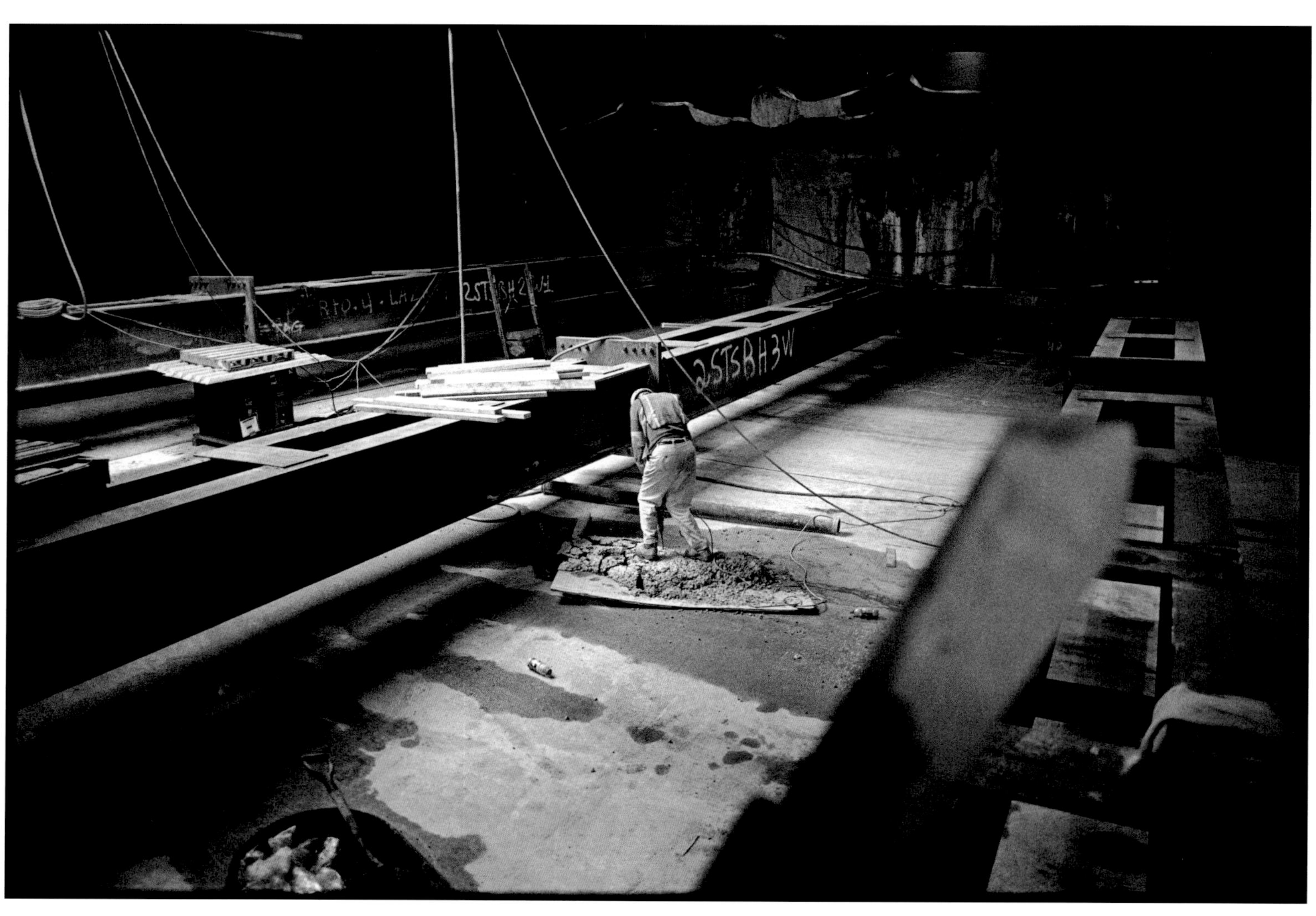

Under Summer Street
2003

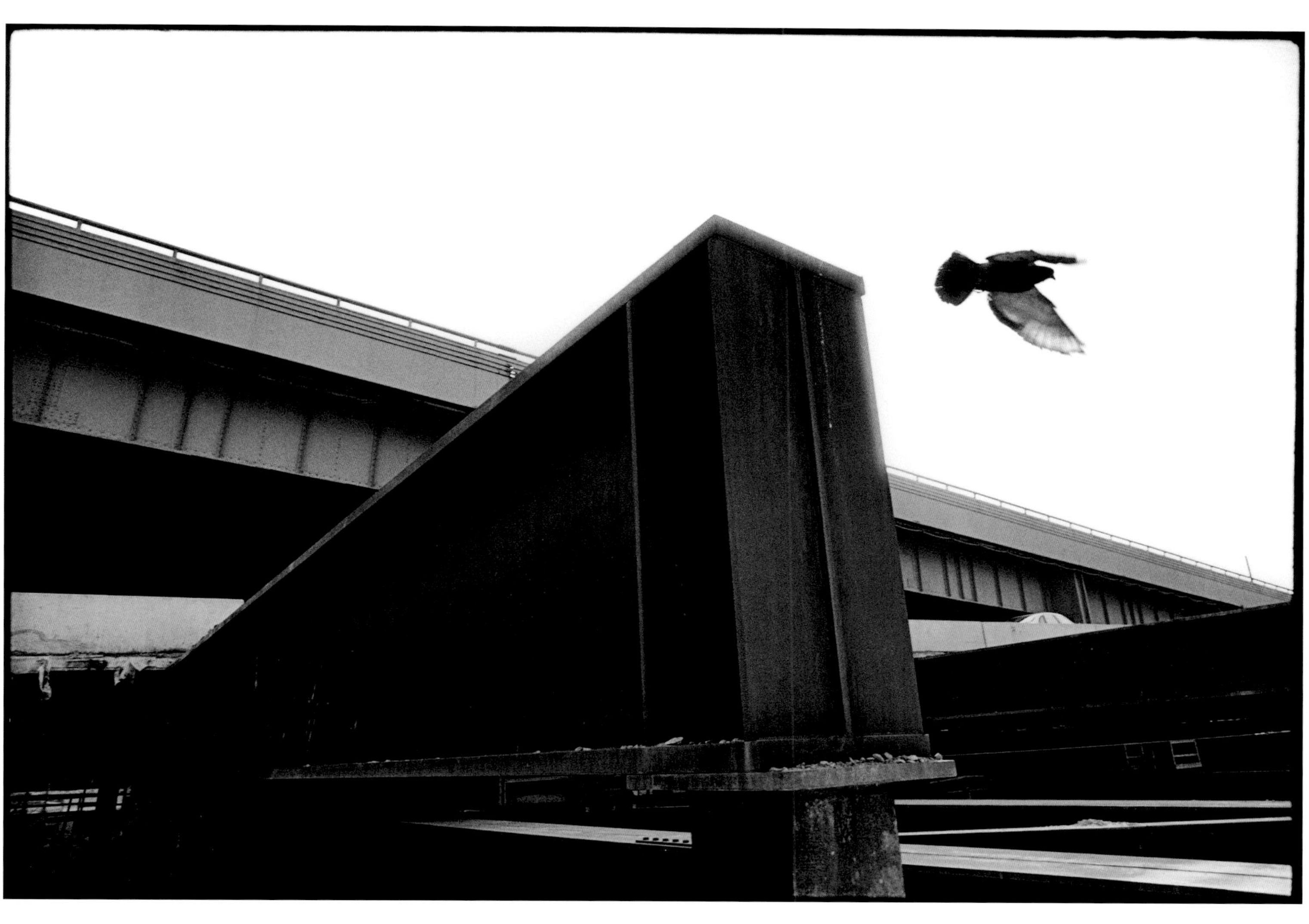

Support beam near
North Station Green Line stop
2001

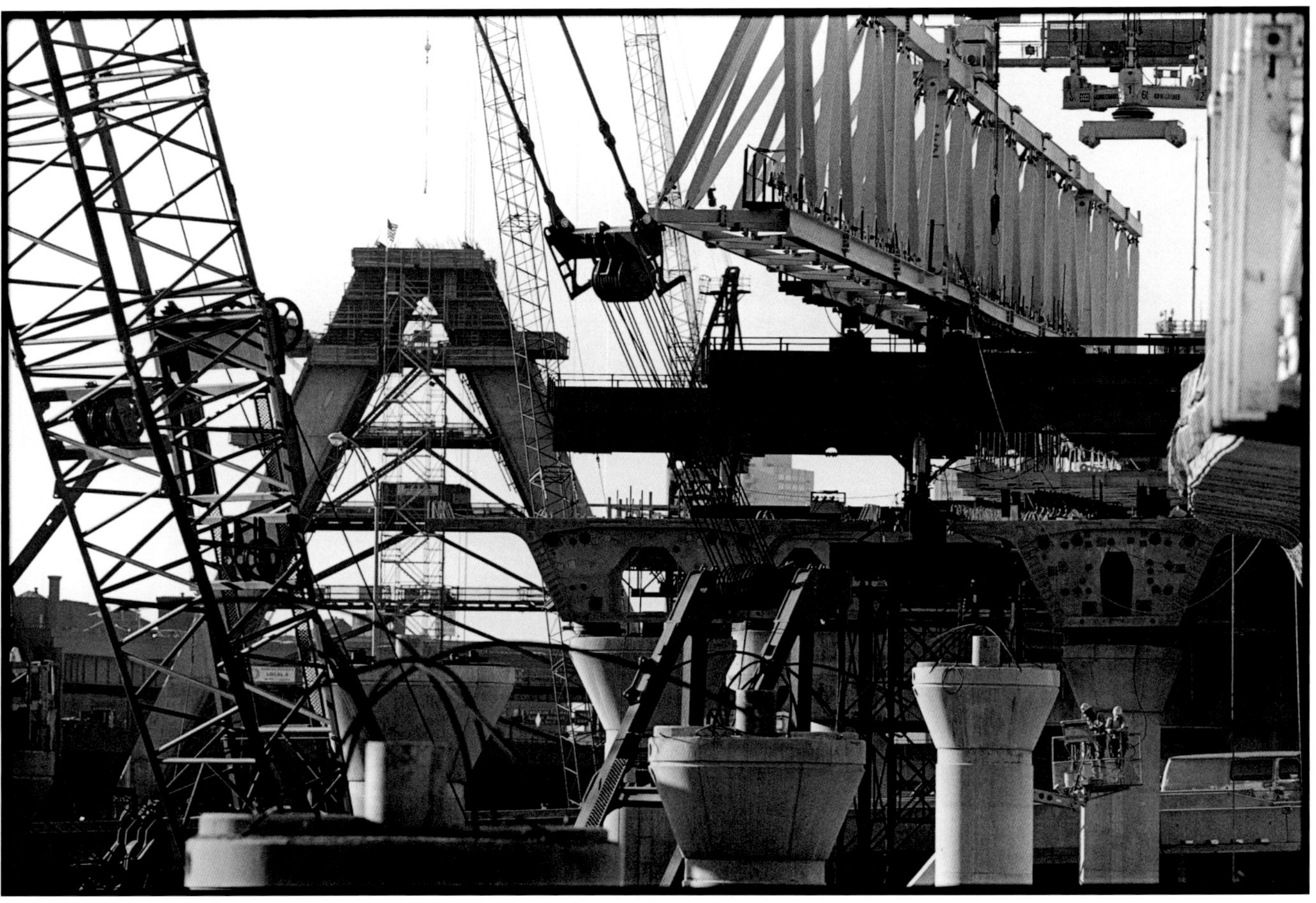

Acknowledgments

I want to extend my gratitude to Nubar Alexanian, who helped very early on to restore my vision; it's made all the difference. Thanks to Costa Manos, who has always given me honest and candid direction; and to Roswell Angier, for being in my corner from the beginning. For giving me the early amulets I have carried on this journey, deepest gratitude to Bill Burke, my first and best teacher. Special thanks to my parents, Patsy and Jim Hintlian, for their constant love and faith in me; to Carolyn Crimmins Hintlian for her love, understanding, and sturdiness; to John Dore for now; to Arthur LeBrasseur for our intensity; to Jay Hurley and Robert Banks, who both understood and supported this work from the beginning; to Paul McNally, Martin Walsh, Michael Monahan, and Tom Harrington, who trusted and understood the big picture; and to Jim Coyle, who introduced me to the high steel. To Roger Warner for the right moment. Thank you to Sherry Krauter, Brenda Olesin, and the entire Leica Camera Service Department, for keeping my cameras running. It is my honor to thank Fred Salvucci for his words here and for his early encouragement of this work. Thanks to Nina Talayco for insight beyond; to Steve Bridges for the design and his steady spirit; and to Webster and Katie Bull for really getting it.

My deepest appreciation to the workers of the Central Artery/Tunnel Project, who were my guides and protectors. Without their help, this work would not have been possible.

The following organizations are acknowledged for their support in this project:
Aztec Steel Corporation
Carpenters' District Council of New England
International Brotherhood of Electrical Workers Local 103
Iron Workers District Council of New England
Iron Workers District Council of New England – LMCT Safety Department
Laborers Local 223
Iron Workers Local 7
Iron Workers Local 7 Joint Apprenticeship Committee Fund
J. F. White Construction Company
The Leavitt Corporation
Massachusetts Laborers' District Council
Modern Continental Company
Prime Steel Corporation
Regis Steel Corporation
South Shore Rebar
Trevilcos Corporation

Michael Hintlian

◄ South tower of the Zakim Bridge and gantry crane
1999

Highway segments, viaducts south of South Station
2002

Michael Hintlian was born in Boston. He earned his bachelor of fine arts degree from the School of the Museum of Fine Arts and Tufts University, and a master's degree in business administration from Cornell University. He is a full-time documentary photographer whose work has been published in major U.S. publications and widely exhibited. He lives in Ipswich, Massachusetts.

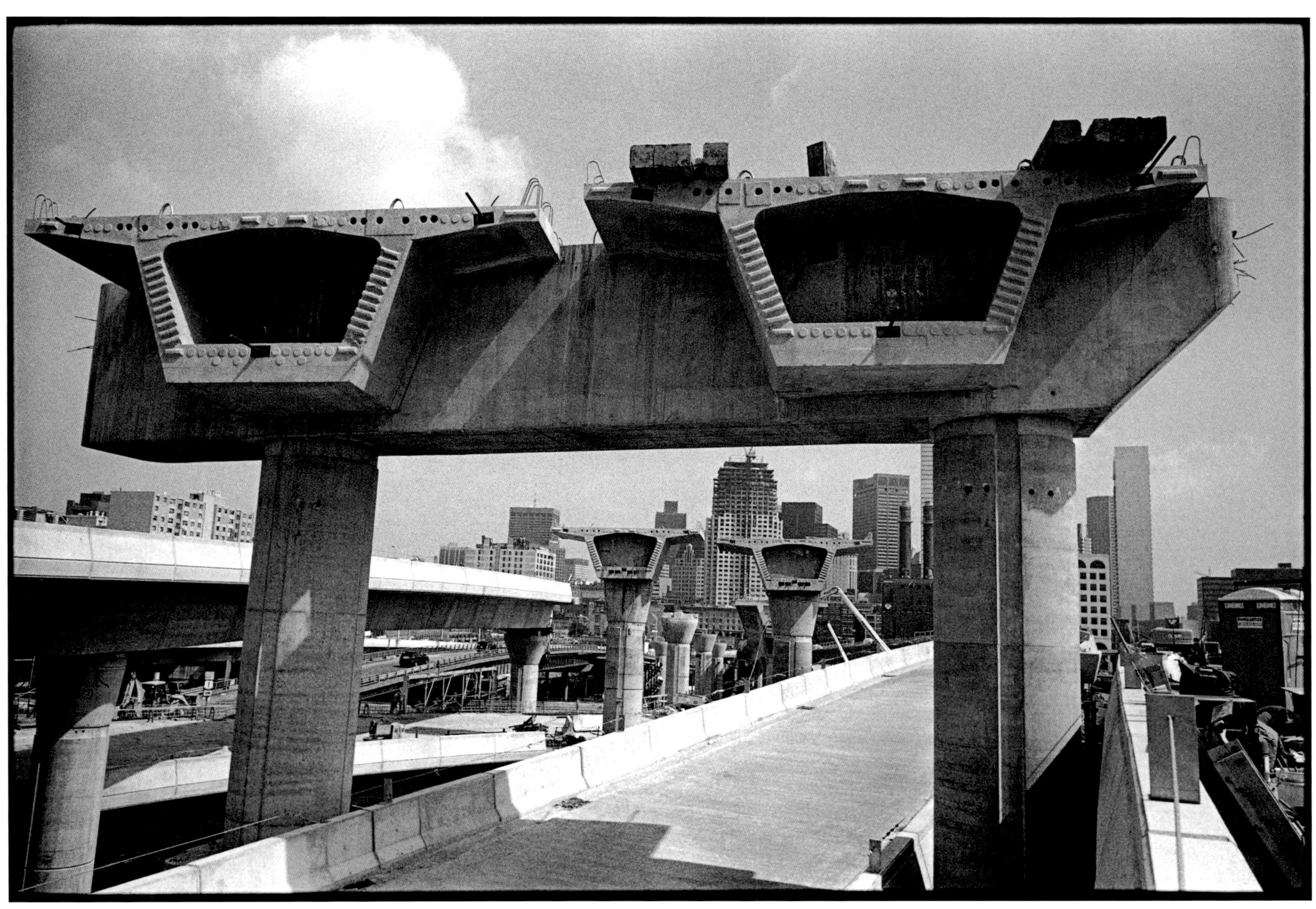